ROCK & ROLL

TRIVIA QUIZ BOOK

VOLUME 2

400 ROCK TRIVIA QUESTIONS
(1950s–1960s)

*an encyclopedia of rock & roll's
trivia-information

in question/answer format*

email comments/corrections: rocknrolltriviaquizbook.com
(808) 261–6666

VOLUME 2-- Updated 2019 ed.

Love, Presley

ROCK & ROLL TRIVIA QUIZ BOOK Vol. 2

(128 pages)

1. Rock-&-Roll Quiz Book   I. Love, Presley   II. Title: Rock and Roll

2. Music

COVER DESIGN: *Doug Behrens*

ISBN: 978–1984952004

Printed In The United States of America

----

text collection by: **Presley Love**
format/production by: Raymond Karelitz

The Legacy of Presley Love

In 1992, music-aficionado Presley Love compiled a vast treasure of rock & roll lyric-memoribilia, including songs from the earliest days of rock & roll up through the late '80s. This musical quiz-format collection lay dormant except for the release of a single volume which contained 400 questions. The original book — printed in 1992 — became, over the years, an Amazon.com favorite, with very positive response from those who loved the book for its "party-flavor" appeal.

In 2014, the entire vault of Presley Love's music-lyric memoribilia was located in a storage locker — containing his collection of lyric-questions and trivia questions in quiz format! After four years of diligent compiling and organizing, the entire Presley Love collection of rock lyrics, rock titles and rock group trivia is now available in quiz-format!

We are proud to unveil the exciting 6-volume set of Presley Love's *ROCK TRIVIA QUIZ BOOKS 1950s-1960s,* including amazing and little-known facts from the rock era of the '50s & '60s. We hope you enjoy these fabulous party-favorites in quiz-format, books guaranteed to amuse, entertain and inform!

If you're brave enough to test your skills,
here's a simple SCORING CHART:

(questions are worth 1 point each — "Harder Questions" are worth 2 points each . . . If you are able to correctly answer the question without the three choices, you receive twice the point value!)

If you score . . .

20+ Points: You probably STILL think it's 1965!
(Check your wardrobe!)

16–19: You probably paid more attention to
rock & roll than books & school!
(Check your report card!)

11–15: There's a lot of rock & roll memories
in your blood!

6–10: Don't you wish you'd listened more closely
to rock & roll ?!
(It's never too late to be hip!)

0–5: Where were YOU when rock began to rule ?!
*(Time to get experienced —
run to your music store now!!!)*

ROCK TRIVIA QUESTIONS

Quiz 1

1. Which artist spent the most consecutive weeks in the U.S. Billboard Top 100 singles-chart during the 1950s & 1960s ?
   a. Pat Boone
   b. Elvis Presley
   c. Johnny Mathis

****

2. Who provided backing instrumentals on the Everly Brothers' 1959 song *('Til) I Kissed You* ?
   a. Duane Eddy
   b. the Crickets
   c. the Champs

****

3. Who gave Chubby Checker his stage-name ?
   a. Fats Domino
   b. Dick Clark's wife
   c. Berry Gordy

****

4. What is Little Richard's full name ?
   a. Ricard LeJardin
   b. Ricardo Lamont
   c. Richard Penniman

5. Who originally recorded *Singing the Blues,* a #1 hit for Guy Mitchell in 1956 ?

    a. George Hamilton IV
    b. Marty Robbins
    c. Johnny Cash

****

6. Which of the following was NOT a member of the Falcons, whose song *You're So Fine* hit the rock charts in 1959 ?

    a. Wilson Pickett
    b. Otis Redding
    c. Eddie Floyd

****

7. How did teen sensation Frankie Lymon die ?

    a. in a plane crash
    b. from a drug overdose
    c. he was struck by lightning

****

8. What objection did Pat Boone have in recording Fats Domino's *Ain't That a Shame* ?

    a. he felt it unfair to copy the song
       just to satisfy the white audience
    b. he didn't like the title's grammatical error
    c. he preferred to have a backup band

9. What was Frankie Avalon's real (birth) name ?

      a. Francis Cellini

      b. Franco Avaliere

      c. Francis Avallone

****

10. On which label did Del Shannon record his hits, including *Runaway* ?

      a. Big Top

      b. Gee

      c. Smash

****

11. Which group featured members including Angelo, Freddie and Carlo ?

      a. the Belmonts

      b. the Elegants

      c. the Four Seasons

****

Questions 12-16: SONG HITS

12. What was Jerry Lee Lewis's last U.S. Top 20 hit ?

      a. *Whole Lot of Shakin' Going On*

      b. *Great Balls of Fire*

      c. *Breathless*

13. Which of the following hits charted highest for Nat "King" Cole on the U.S. Billboard singles chart ?

    a. *A Blossom Fell*

    b. *Ramblin' Rose*

    c. *Those Lazy–Hazy–Crazy Days of Summer*

****

14. What was the Everly Brothers' first U.S. #1 hit ?

    a. *Cathy's Clown*

    b. *All I Have To Do Is Dream*

    c. *Wake Up Little Susie*

****

15. What was the Ronettes' last U.S. Top 40 hit ?

    a. *Walking In the Rain*

    b. *Baby, I Love You*

    c. *Do I Love You?*

****

16. What was Ray Peterson's first U.S. Billboard Top 40 hit ?

    a. *Corinna, Corinna*

    b. *Tell Laura I Love Her*

    c. *The Wonder of You*

17. On what show did Gene Vincent & the Blue Caps make their first national television appearance ?

      a. The Perry Como Show

      b. Toast of the Town

      c. The Big Beat

****

18. Who actually sang on the 1958 hit *Jennie Lee* ?

      a. Jan and Dean

      b. Jan and Arnie

      c. Jan, Arnie and Dean

****

19. What was the first pop single record that Sam Cooke released ?

      a. Lovable

      b. You Send Me

      c. I'll Come Running Back to You

****

20. Sam Phillips, early Elvis promoter through his Sun Records label, sold his interest to RCA Records in 1955. But he went on to make much more money investing in a fledgling company. What was this company ?

      a. Microsoft

      b. McDonald's

      c. Holiday Inn

Quiz 1

1. a. Pat Boone . . . 169 weeks — in 2nd is Elvis Presley with 131 weeks
2. b. the Crickets
3. b. Dick Clark's wife . . . actually, his nickname already was "Chubby" . . . Dick's wife Bobbie Clark simply added "Checker" to complete the humorous takeoff on Fats Domino
4. c. Richard Penniman
5. b. Marty Robbins
6. b. Otis Redding
7. b. from a drug overdose, in 1968
8. b. he didn't like the title's grammatical error — he wanted to change the lyric and title to *Isn't It a Shame*
9. c. Francis Avallone
10. a. Big Top
11. a. the Belmonts

****
Questions 12-16: SONG HITS
12. c. *Breathless*
13. b. *Ramblin' Rose,* #2 for 2 weeks in 1962
14. c. *Wake Up Little Susie*
15. a. *Walking In the Rain*
16. c. *The Wonder of You*

****
Questions 17-20: HARDER QUESTIONS
17. a. *The Perry Como Show,* on July 28, 1955
18. c. Jan, Arnie and Dean . . . Although Dean Torrence was in the Army at the time of the single's release, he actually recorded it with Jan Berry . . . Arnie Ginsberg provided additional background vocals . . . the Jan & Arnie label is therefore not fully correct; it would have been more accurate for the label to read: "Jan & Dean, with Arnie"
19. a. *Lovable,* recorded for Specialty Records under the name Dale Cooke, in 1957
20. c. Holiday Inn — the hotel chain

Quiz 2

1. Who was Elvis Presley's long-time manager ?

        a. Colonel Tom Parker

        b. Brian Epstein

        c. Sid Bernstein

****

2. Who was the first white girl-group to reach #1 on the U.S. Billboard singles chart ?

        a. the Jaynetts

        b. the Angels

        c. the Chordettes

****

3. Who recorded *Blue Velvet* a decade before Bobby Vinton's version in 1963 topped the U.S. singles chart for three weeks ?

        a. the Five Satins

        b. the Clovers

        c. the Platters

****

4. What song was released as a follow-up to the 1956 Heartbeats song *A Thousand Miles Away* ?

        a. *Working My Way Back to You*

        b. *Daddy's Home*

        c. *Mr. Lonely*

5. What was Sam Cooke's early backup band called ?

      a. the Soul Stirrers

      b. the Troubadours

      c. the Rhythm Aces

****

6. What #1 hit from the '50s & '60s stayed in the Top 40 U.S. record charts for the longest period of time ?

      a. *The Twist* / Chubby Checker

      b. *Mack the Knife* / Bobby Darin

      c. *Rock Around the Clock* / Bill Haley & His Comets

****

7. What was the 1958 Elvis Presley movie *King Creole* originally titled ?

      a. *King of the Garden Orchids*

      b. *A Glove in the Ring*

      c. *A Stone for Danny Fisher*

****

8. What early rock 'n' roll group group featured lead singers Charlie White and Buddy Bailey ?

      a. the Midnighters

      b. the Clovers

      c. the Penguins

9. Which group featured members including Herb, Tony, David and Zola ?

> a. the Platters
>
> b. the Tune Weavers
>
> c. the Elegants

****

10. Walden Robert Cassoto was the real (birth) name for which of the following '60s stars ?

> a. Tony Orlando
>
> b. Bobby Rydell
>
> c. Bobby Darin

****

11. On which label did the Everly Brothers record their earliest hits, including *Wake Up Little Susie* ?

> a. Cadence
>
> b. Keen
>
> c. Kapp

****

Questions 12-16: SONG HITS

12. What was Roy Orbison's first single to reach the U.S. Billboard Top 20 record charts ?

> a. *Dream Baby*
>
> b. *Only the Lonely*
>
> c. *Oh, Pretty Woman*

13. Which of the following hits charted highest for Marty Robbins on the U.S. Billboard singles chart ?

    a. *Devil Woman*

    b. *El Paso*

    c. *A White Sport Coat (And a Pink Carnation)*

****

14. What was Steve Lawrence's only U.S. #1 hit ?

    a. *Pretty Blue Eyes*

    b. *Go Away Little Girl*

    c. *Portrait of My Love*

****

15. What was the Shirelles' first Billboard Hot 100 hit single ?

    a. *Tonight's the Night*

    b. *Will You Love Me Tomorrow*

    c. *I Met Him On a Sunday*

****

16. What was Frankie Avalon's first single to reach the U.S. Billboard Top 20 record charts ?

    a. *Dede Dinah*

    b. *Venus*

    c. *Why*

HARDER QUESTIONS (17-20): 2 points each
(4 points if you can answer the question without the three choices !)

17. What was the name of the group that Clyde McPhatter merged with, forming the first incarnation of the Drifters ?

    a. the Honeylovers

    b. the Civitones

    c. the Magnificents

****

18. Who was the backup group in Jerry Wallace's 1959 hit *Primrose Lane* ?

    a. the Primettes

    b. the Clovers

    c. the Jewels

****

19. On what show did Elvis Presley make his network television premiere ?

    a. *Tommy & Jimmy Dorsey's Stage Show*

    b. *The Toast of the Town*

    c. *The Les Crane Show*

****

20. What was Chuck Berry's 1955 hit *Maybellene* named after ?

    a. a perfume

    b. a former girlfriend

    c. a cow

Quiz 2

1. a. Colonel Tom Parker
2. b. the Angels, in 1963
3. b. the Clovers, who recorded it in 1954
4. b. *Daddy's Home,* a 1961 hit by Shep & the Limelites, with lead singer James Sheppard — who also, incidentally, was the lead singer for the Heartbeats hit . . . in the final line he sings, "I'm not a thousand miles away"
5. a. the Soul Stirrers, a gospel group
6. c. *Rock Around the Clock* / Bill Haley & His Comets, reaching #1 in 1955, spending 29 weeks on the charts — and re-released in 1974, staying on the charts for another 14 weeks: 43 weeks total!
7. c. *A Stone for Danny Fisher,* the name of the novel on which the movie was based
8. b. the Clovers
9. a. the Platters
10. c. Bobby Darin
11. a. Cadence

****

Questions 12-16: SONG HITS

12. b. *Only the Lonely,* in 1960
13. b. *El Paso,* #1 for 2 weeks in 1960
14. b. *Go Away Little Girl*
15. c. *I Met Him On a Sunday,* released in 1957 on Tiara Records
16. a. *Dede Dinah,* in February, 1958

****

Questions 17-20: HARDER QUESTIONS

17. b. the Civitones . . . the early-Drifters hits included *Money Honey* (1953) and *Honey Love* (1954)
18. c. the Jewels, which included '70s singer Al Wilson
19. a. *Tommy & Jimmy Dorsey's Stage Show*
20. c. a cow, as featured in a children's story . . . the tune itself was from an old country song

Quiz 3

1. Elvis Presley recorded five songs during a furlough from the Army. Which of the following songs from that recording session was NOT released until after he was discharged ?

    a. *I Got Stung*

    b. *A Big Hunk of Love*

    c. *(Now and Then There's) A Fool Such As I*

****

2. Who was known as the "Mighty Double-D" ?

    a. Dicky Doo & the Don'ts

    b. Dion

    c. Dick & Dee Dee

****

3. Who originally turned down the offer to release *Mr. Blue*, the 1959 #1 hit for the Fleetwoods ?

    a. the Everly Brothers

    b. the Platters

    c. Ricky Nelson

****

4. Why did the manager of singer Gary Anderson promote him as "U.S. Bonds" ?

a. so that he could get government support for overseas gigs

b. so that fans would know that he was not from British soil

c. so that he was able to incorporate the slogan "buy U.S. Bonds"

5. Who did boxing legend Cassius Clay (Muhammad Ali) call "the world's greatest rock 'n' roll singer — the greatest singer in the world" ?

      a. Smokey Robinson

      b. Little Richard

      c. Sam Cooke

****

6. What controversial movie did *Rock Around the Clock* first appear in that resulted in a #1 hit for Bill Haley and His Comets ?

      a. *Go Johnny Go!*

      b. *Blackboard Jungle*

      c. *Rock Around the Clock*

****

7. Who did Jerry Lee Lewis marry in 1958, an event that severely damaged his music career ?

      a. his thirteen–year–old cousin

      b. his manager's daughter

      c. an avowed atheist

****

8. What was the only rock & roll movie that Ritchie Valens appeared in ?

      a. *Don't Knock the Rock*

      b. *Go Johnny Go!*

      c. *Rock, Rock, Rock*

9. In what movie did Bobby Rydell's 1960 hit *Swingin' School* appear ?

> a. *Because They're Young*
> b. *Go Johnny Go!*
> c. *Senior Prom*

****

10. On which label did Elvis Presley record his biggest hits, including *Jailhouse Rock* ?

> a. RCA
> b. Coral
> c. Liberty

****

11. Which group featured members including Ron, Rudy and O'Kelly ?

> a. the O'Jays
> b. the Isley Brothers
> c. the Del-Vikings

****

Questions 12-16: SONG HITS

12. What was Jimmie Rodgers' only U.S. #1 hit ?

> a. *Secretly*
> b. *Kisses Sweeter Than Wine*
> c. *Honeycomb*

13. Which of the following hits charted highest for the Shirelles on the U.S. Billboard singles chart ?

> a. *Will You Love Me Tomorrow*
>
> b. *Soldier Boy*
>
> c. *Dedicated To the One I Love*

****

14. What was the Drifters' last U.S. Top 40 hit ?

> a. *On Broadway*
>
> b. *Under the Boardwalk*
>
> c. *Saturday Night At the Movies*

****

15. What was Buddy Holly's first U.S. Billboard Hot 100 hit ?

> a. *Maybe Baby*
>
> b. *Peggy Sue*
>
> c. *That'll Be the Day*

****

16. Though no other song by Mark Dinning reached the U.S. Top 40 singles chart, what song did he take all the way to #1?

> a. *Last Kiss*
>
> b. *Teen Angel*
>
> c. *Tell Laura I Love Her*

HARDER QUESTIONS (17-20): 2 points each
(4 points if you can answer the question without the three choices !)

17. In what hotel did Elvis Presley make his Las Vegas debut ?

> a. the Frontier Hotel
> b. the Stardust Casino
> c. the Golden Nugget

****

18. In their earliest days, what name did Buddy Holly's band record under ?

> a. Buddy Holly & the Three Tunes
> b. the Chirping Chords
> c. the Hollywood Four

****

19. Which of the following was NOT one of the guests on Alan Freed's television show, *The Big Beat* ?

> a. Buddy Holly
> b. Guy Mitchell
> c. the Del-Vikings

****

20. How did the Champs of *Tequila* fame derive their group's name ?

> a. from a brand of whiskey
> b. from a blues song
> c. from the name of a horse

Quiz 3

1. a. *I Got Stung*
2. b. Dion (Dion DiMucci)
3. b. the Platters
4. c. so that he was able to incorporate the slogan "buy U.S. Bonds"
5. c. Sam Cooke
6. b. *Blackboard Jungle* ... it played at the 1955 movie's introduction ... the movie *Rock Around the Clock* was released in 1956
7. a. his thirteen-year-old cousin
8. b. *Go Johnny Go!*
9. a. *Because They're Young*
10. a. RCA
11. b. the Isley Brothers

****

Questions 12-16: SONG HITS

12. c. *Honeycomb*
13. b. *Soldier Boy,* #1 for 3 weeks in 1962, 1 week longer than *Will You Love Me Tomorrow*
14. c. *Saturday Night At the Movies*
15. c. *That'll Be the Day*
16. b. *Teen Angel,* in 1959

****

Questions 17-20: HARDER QUESTIONS

17. a. the Frontier Hotel, on April 22, 1956
18. a. Buddy Holly & the Three Tunes
19. a. Buddy Holly
20. c. from the name of a horse . . . The label on which they recorded, Challenge, was owned by cowboy Gene Autry, whose cherished horse was named "Champion"

Quiz 4

1. From the lyrics of what song did retro-'50s group Sha Na Na get their name ?
   - a. *Get a Job*
   - b. *Runaround Sue*
   - c. *Who Put the Bomp*

****

2. What was Lloyd Price's nickname ?
   - a. "Stagger Lee"
   - b. "Mr. Personality"
   - c. "Mr. Soul"

****

3. Which group released a cover version of the Hollywood Argyles' *Alley-Oop* and released it at the same time as the original version ?
   - a. Buchanan & Goodman
   - b. the Rinky-Dinks
   - c. Dante & the Evergreens

****

4. What was Brenda Lee affectionately called ?
   - a. "America's Sweetheart"
   - b. "The '50s Teen Queen"
   - c. "Little Miss Dynamite"

5. Which of the following songs was also written by *Tossin' & Turnin'* writer Ritchie Adams ?

     a. *Tonight You Belong To Me*

     b. *You Were Mine*

     c. *Mr. Lee*

****

6. Which of the following rockers did the Jordainaires NOT back up ?

     a. Ral Donner

     b. Jack Scott

     c. Ricky Nelson

****

7. Which of the following artists first released the single *Devil or Angel* ?

     a. Bobby Vee

     b. the Clovers

     c. the Graduates

****

8. What did Chuck Berry originally want to become professionally before he became a professional musician ?

     a. a talent agent

     b. a movie star

     c. a hairdresser

9. What Elvis Presley movie did *Puppet On a String* appear in ?

        a. *Wild In the Country*

        b. *Double Trouble*

        c. *Girl Happy*

****

10. On which label did Claudine Clark record her hit *Party Lights* ?

        a. Chancellor

        b. Parkway

        c. Argo

****

11. Charles Westover was the real (birth) name for which of the following rock stars ?

        a. Del Shannon

        b. Bobby Vee

        c. Fabian

****

Questions 12-16: SONG HITS

12. What was Roy Orbison's first U.S. #1 hit ?

        a. *Oh, Pretty Woman*

        b. *Crying*

        c. *Running Scared*

13. Which of the following hits charted highest for Martha & the Vandellas on the U.S. Billboard singles chart ?

> a. *Dancing In the Street*
>
> b. *Heat Wave*
>
> c. *Quicksand*

****

14. What was Dee Clark's last U.S. Top 40 hit ?

> a. *Raindrops*
>
> b. *Your Friends*
>
> c. *How About That*

****

15. What was Bryan Hyland's only U.S. #1 hit ?

> a. *Gypsy Woman*
>
> b. *Sealed With a Kiss*
>
> c. *Itsy Bitsy Teenie Weenie Yellow Polka-Dot Bikini*

****

16. What was Chuck Berry's last single to chart in the Top 40 ?

> a. *My Ding-A-Ling*
>
> b. *Reelin' & Rockin'*
>
> c. *No Particular Place to Go*

HARDER QUESTIONS (17-20): 2 points each
(4 points if you can answer the question without the three choices !)

17. Who was '50s rock star Jack Scott's backup band ?

> a. the Chantones
>
> b. the Dolphins
>
> c. the Starfires

****

18. What was a former name for the Chiffons ?

> a. the Sweethearts
>
> b. the Chicago Trio
>
> c. the Love Letters

****

19. Actor Bert Convy was once a member of which '50s group ?

> a. the Hilltoppers
>
> b. the Cheers
>
> c. the Four Aces

****

20. Which of the following '60s rock stars was originally asked to record *The Twist* for *Dick Clark's American Bandstand* ?

> a. Len Barry
>
> b. Freddy Cannon
>
> c. Paul Anka

answers

Quiz 4

1. a. *Get a Job,* the Silhouettes' 1957 hit
2. b. "Mr. Personality"
3. c. Dante & the Evergreens . . . their version reached #15, while the Hollywood Argyles' version reached #1
4. c. "Little Miss Dynamite"
5. b. *You Were Mine,* a 1959 Top 40 hit by the Fireflies
6. b. Jack Scott
7. b. the Clovers, in 1956
8. c. a hairdresser
9. c. *Girl Happy*
10. a. Chancellor
11. a. Del Shannon

****

Questions 12-16: SONG HITS

12. c. *Running Scared*
13. a. *Dancing In the Street,* #2 in 1964
14. a. *Raindrops*
15. c. *Itsy Bitsy Teenie Weenie Yellow Polka-Dot Bikini*
16. b. *Reelin' & Rockin',* the live version reaching #27 in 1973

****

Questions 17-20: HARDER QUESTIONS

17. a. the Chantones
18. a. the Sweethearts
19. b. the Cheers, whose hit *Black Denim Trousers* was a Top 10 hit in 1955
20. b. Freddy Cannon . . . Dick Clark did not feel that the original Hank Ballard recording would fit into the show's target audience . . . But Freddy Cannon nevertheless turned down the invitation because his hit *Way Down Yonder in New Orleans* was climbing the charts. He later regretted his decision but added that anyone could have made it a hit because it was such a good song . . . Dick Clark found his star-to-be (Chubby Checker) shortly thereafter, and "the rest is history"

-24-

Quiz 5

1. Who was the oldest singer to have a #1 U.S. single ?
   a. Walter Brennan
   b. Louis Armstrong
   c. Bing Crosby

****

2. Which of the following singers was unhappy with his recording stage name ?
   a. Lou Christie
   b. Bobby Vee
   c. Ernie K–Doe

****

3. What was the slogan for the early '60s label Miracle Records ?
   a. "there's nothing like a miracle"
   b. "we make miracles happen"
   c. "if it's a hit, it's a miracle"

****

4. Who was the actual non–Crystals lead singer on the Crystals' hit *He's a Rebel* ?
   a. Martha Reeves
   b. Shirley Jackson
   c. Darlene Love

5. What is unique about Neil Sedaka's song *Breaking Up Is Hard to Do* ?

    a. it was the only song to climb the charts on four different record labels

    b. it was the only song released twice that became more successful the second time on the chart

    c. it was the only song to be recorded by the same artist twice and reach the Top 10 twice

****

6. Who wrote Buddy Holly's final top 40 hit, *It Doesn't Matter Anymore* ?

    a. Bobby Vee

    b. Paul Anka

    c. The Big Bopper

****

7. Which of his many hits did Pat Boone reportedly consider his favorite ?

    a. *Speedy Gonzales*

    b. *Moody River*

    c. *Love Letters In the Sand*

****

8. On which label did Connie Francis record her biggest hits, including *Lipstick On Your Collar* ?

    a. MGM

    b. Fury

    c. Warner Brothers

9. What was Bobby Rydell's real (birth) name ?

      a. Robert Marconi

      b. Robert Ridarelli

      c. Julian Ryder

****

10. Which group featured members including Kathy, Georgeanna, Wanda and Gladys ?

      a. the Marvelettes

      b. the Cookies

      c. the Crystals

****

11. On which label did the Four Seasons record their hits, including *Sherry* ?

      a. Philips

      b. Valiant

      c. Vee–Jay

****

Questions 12-16: SONG HITS

12. What was Jack Scott's last U.S. Top 20 hit ?

      a. *What In the World's Come Over You*

      b. *Burning Bridges*

      c. *Goodbye Baby*

13. Which of the following hits charted highest for Little Anthony & the Imperials on the U.S. Billboard singles chart ?

        a. *Shimmy Shimmy Ko–Ko–Bop*

        b. *Tears On My Pillow*

        c. *Goin' Out Of My Head*

****

14. What was Sue Thompson's first U.S. Billboard Top 40 hit ?

        a. *Sad Movies (Make Me Cry)*

        b. *Norman*

        c. *Paper Tiger*

****

15. Which of the following hits charted highest for Barbara Lewis on the U.S. Billboard singles chart ?

        a. *Make Me Your Baby*

        b. *Baby I'm Yours*

        c. *Hello Stranger*

****

16. What was the Coasters' first Top 20 hit ?

        a. *Charlie Brown*

        b. *Yakety Yak*

        c. *Searchin'*

17. Who often filled in for any absent Shirelles member during their busy concert schedule ?

      a. Dionne Warwick

      b. Little Eva

      c. Barbara Lewis

****

18. What song did Dick Clark promote on his *American Bandstand* television show by offering the single in exchange for 5 Beechnut gum wrappers and 50¢ ?

      a. *Palisades Park*

      b. *Breathless*

      c. *The Twist*

****

19. Who suggested the name change for singer Connie Francis ?

      a. Arthur Godfrey

      b. Mitch Miller

      c. Pat Boone

****

20. Eddie Cochran teamed with Hank Cochran in 1955, billing themselves as the Cochran Brothers. What relationship did the two share ?

      a. they were actually brothers

      b. they were second cousins

      c. they weren't related

Quiz 5

1. b. **Louis Armstrong,** with *Hello Dolly,* in 1964 — he was 63 years old
2. a. **Lou Christie** . . . Lugee Sacco, leader of Lugee & the Lions, was unaware of his "new name" until he saw it on his first single for C&C Records, *The Gypsy Cried*
3. c. **"if it's a hit, it's a miracle"**
4. c. **Darlene Love, along with her group, the Blossoms** . . . As recalled by Darlene Love, the Crystals "had a falling out" with producer Phil Spector, who wanted to have the song recorded — and because the Crystals had moved to New York while she was living in Los Angeles, the city where the studio was located, she was chosen by Spector to record the song. Incidentally, once the song became a national hit, the Crystals had to learn the song to sing on their tours !
5. c. **it was the only song to be recorded by the same artist twice and reach the Top 10 twice**
6. b. **Paul Anka**
7. a. *Speedy Gonzales*
8. a. **MGM**
9. b. **Robert Ridarelli**
10. a. **the Marvelettes**
11. c. **Vee–Jay**

****

Questions 12-16: SONG HITS

12. b. *Burning Bridges*
13. b. *Tears On My Pillow,* reaching #4 in 1958
14. a. *Sad Movies (Make Me Cry)*
15. c. *Hello Stranger,* reaching #3 in 1963
16. c. *Searchin',* along with the flip side, *Young Blood*

****

Questions 17-20: HARDER QUESTIONS

17. a. **Dionne Warwick,** who, as with the Shirelles, was on the Scepter Records label
18. b. *Breathless,* successfully promoted for Jerry Lee Lewis in 1958 . . . it also stimulated Beechnut Gum sales !
19. a. **Arthur Godfrey,** after she appeared on his talent show in 1955
20. c. **they weren't related** . . . Eddie Cochran's actual last name was Cochrane, from which he dropped the "e" when the group formed . . .

Quiz 6

1. In what sport was actor/singer Tab Hunter considered an amateur-professional ?
   a. baseball
   b. ice-skating
   c. fencing

****

2. What was the title of a 1962 parody to Jimmy Dean's *Big Bad John* ?
   a. *Short Fat Fannie*
   b. *Small Sad Sam*
   c. *A Helluva Woman*

****

3. In *Big Bad John,* the last line of the song was changed to "At the bottom of this mine lies a big, big man". What was the original final line in the original release, before it was pulled and replaced ?
   a. "At the bottom of this mine lies a true American".
   b. "At the bottom of this mine lies one helluva man".
   c. "At the bottom of this mine is the future of mankind".

****

4. What song was released as an "answer" to Gene Chandler's 1962 hit *The Duke of Earl* ?
   a. *The Duchess of Earl*
   b. *Walking With the Duke*
   c. *I Married the Duke of Earl*

5. What was the real (birth) name for '50s *Rockin' Robin* rocker Bobby Day ?

      a. Robert Byrd

      b. Robert Jackson

      c. Robert Sarno

****

6. Who was the youngest singer to reach the top of the U.S. singles chart in the rock era of the '50s – '80s ?

      a. Frankie Avalon

      b. Paul Anka

      c. Stevie Wonder

****

7. Who wrote the Connie Francis hit *Where the Boys Are* ?

      a. Neil Sedaka

      b. Lesley Gore

      c. Carole King

****

8. What was the original name of the Marketts hit instrumental *Out of Limits* ?

      a. *Twilight Zone*

      b. *Outer Limits*

      c. *One Step Beyond*

9. On which label did Shelley Fabares record her hits, including *Johnny Angel*?

> **a. Colpix**
>
> **b. Miracle**
>
> **c. Hickory**

****

10. Which group featured members including Ed, George, Leroy and Ronald ?

> **a. the Temptations**
>
> **b. the Miracles**
>
> **c. Ruby & the Romantics**

****

11. What movie did Paul Anka's *Lonely Boy* first appear in ?

> **a. *Girls Town***
>
> **b. *Teenage Caveman***
>
> **c. *Daddy-O***

****

Questions 12-16: SONG HITS

12. What was Dee Dee Sharp's first U.S. Billboard Top 40 hit ?

> **a. *Gravy (For My Mashed Potatoes)***
>
> **b. *Ride!***
>
> **c. *Mashed Potato Time***

13. What was the Chiffons' last U.S. Top 40 hit ?

   a. *A Love So Fine*

   b. *Sweet Talkin' Guy*

   c. *I Have a Boyfriend*

****

14. What was Bobby Rydell's first U.S. Billboard Top 40 hit ?

   a. *Wild One*

   b. *Kissin' Time*

   c. *We Got Love*

****

15. What was the Dovells' last U.S. Top 40 hit ?

   a. *Hully Gully Baby*

   b. *You Can't Sit Down*

   c. *Bristol Twistin' Annie*

****

16. What was Dion & the Belmonts' first U.S. Billboard Top 40 hit ?

   a. *I Wonder Why*

   b. *Where Or When*

   c. *A Teenager In Love*

HARDER QUESTIONS (17-20): 2 points each

(4 points if you can answer the question without the three choices !)

17. What was reportedly the first instrument that Del Shannon learned to play ?

    a. the guitar

    b. the mellotron

    c. the kazoo

****

18. What local group did Frankie Avalon form with Bobby Rydell while in high school ?

    a. the Philly Prophessionals

    b. the Avallones

    c. Rocco & the Saints

****

19. Which group called themselves the Poquellos when they first formed in high school ?

    a. the Orlons

    b. Dion & the Belmonts

    c. the Shirelles

****

20. What inspired the group name Paul & Paula ?

    a. a newspaper headline

    b. a song title

    c. the first names of the two singers

Quiz 6

1. b. ice-skating
2. b. *Small Sad Sam,* by Phil McLean
3. b. "At the bottom of this mine lies one helluva man"...

   incidentally, the actual title of the earliest original release was *Big John*

4. a. *The Duchess of Earl,* in 1962, by the Pearlettes
5. a. Robert Byrd
6. c. Little Stevie Wonder, who was only 13 when *Fingertips Pt. 2*
   hit #1 in 1963
7. a. Neil Sedaka
8. b. *Outer Limits* ... Due to the popularity of a new weekly sci-fi program
   titled *The Outer Limits* — to which the song had no affiliation — it didn't
   take long before Warner Brothers record company made the legally
   necessary change.
9. a. Colpix
10. c. Ruby & the Romantics ... along with Ruby Nash
11. a. *Girls Town,* a 1959 movie in which Anka appeared, singing the song
    live and accompanying himself on piano

****

Questions 12-16: SONG HITS

12. c. *Mashed Potato Time*
13. b. *Sweet Talkin' Guy,* in 1966
14. b. *Kissin' Time*
15. b. *You Can't Sit Down*
16. a. *I Wonder Why*

****

Questions 17-20: HARDER QUESTIONS

17. c. the kazoo
18. c. Rocco & the Saints
19. c. the Shirelles
20. b. a song title ... "Paul" — the 6'4" Ray Hildebrand — was fixated by
    Annette's song *Tall Paul* when he first began writing *Hey Paula,* soon
    thereafter forming a duo and incorporating the name

Quiz 7

1. Skip & Flip had two hits, *It Was I* and *Cherry Pie,* in 1959/1960. "Flip" was actually Gary Paxton — leader of the *Alley-Oop* Hollywood Argyles — but who was Skip ?

    a. Skip Battin

    b. Phil Spector

    c. Quincy Jones

****

2. What was Elvis Presley's debut hit on RCA Records ?

    a. *Hound Dog*

    b. *Love Me Tender*

    c. *Heartbreak Hotel*

****

3. What 1963 song was inspired by Preston Epps' 1959 Top 40 hit *Bongo Rock* ?

    a. *Hot Pastrami* / Dartells

    b. *Washington Square* / Village Stompers

    c. *Wipe Out* / Surfaris

****

4. What was the real (birth) name of Chipmunks creator David Seville ?

    a. Ross Bagdasarian

    b. David Severino

    c. Zal Verano

5. Between August 8, 1963 and October, 1964, who was the only American musical act to top the British weekly singles chart ?

         a. Lesley Gore

         b. Elvis Presley

         c. Roy Orbison

****

6. What folk group did Glenn Yarbrough, whose hit *Baby The Rain Must Fall* reached #12 in 1965, record with ?

         a. the Limeliters

         b. the Weavers

         c. the New Christy Minstrels

****

7. In what year was *Are You Lonesome Tonight* written ?

         a. 1906

         b. 1926

         c. 1956

****

8. What was the unusual instrument used on Del Shannon's 1961 hit *Runaway* ?

         a. ocarina

         b. mellotron

         c. musitron

9. On which label did the Chiffons record their hits, including *He's So Fine*?

> a. Laurie
>
> b. Fraternity
>
> c. Miracle

****

10. What group were Shirley Owens and Doris Kenner members of?

> a. the Dixie Cups
>
> b. the Shangri-Las
>
> c. the Shirelles

****

11. Which of the following was NOT a member of the Chad Mitchell Trio?

> a. Don Williams
>
> b. John Denver
>
> c. Jim "Roger" McGuinn

****

Questions 12-16: SONG HITS

12. What was Brenda Lee's first U.S. Billboard Top 40 hit?

> a. *I Want to Be Wanted*
>
> b. *Sweet Nothin's*
>
> c. *I'm Sorry*

13. What was Dick & Dee Dee's last U.S. Top 40 hit ?

> a. *Turn Around*
>
> b. *Thou Shalt Not Steal*
>
> c. *Tell Me*

****

14. What was Gary U.S. Bonds' only U.S. #1 hit ?

> a. *Dear Lady Twist*
>
> b. *Quarter to Three*
>
> c. *School Is Out*

****

15. What was James Darren's first U.S. Billboard Top 40 hit ?

> a. *Her Royal Majesty*
>
> b. *Goodbye Cruel World*
>
> c. *Conscience*

****

16. What was Rick Nelson's last U.S. Top 40 hit ?

> a. *Garden Party*
>
> b. *She Belongs to Me*
>
> c. *For You*

HARDER QUESTIONS (17-20): 2 points each
(4 points if you can answer the question without the three choices !)

17. What was a previous name for the group Ruby & the Romantics ?

    a. the Clover Leafs

    b. Ruby & the Runarounds

    c. the Supremes

****

18. Who provided backup vocals for Chubby Checker in his 1960 hit *The Twist* ?

    a. the Orlons

    b. the Dreamlovers

    c. the Dovells

****

19. Which of the following was NOT the "seventh son of a seventh son" ?

    a. Glen Campbell

    b. Donny Osmond

    c. Perry Como

****

20. The Raindrops had a 1963 hit with *The Kind of Boy You Can't Forget.* The group had three people pictured on the album cover, but the group was actually only a duo. Who was the third person pictured ?

    a. a reverse picture of one of the members

    b. a cartoon character

    c. one member's sister

Quiz 7

1. a. Skip Battin, who joined the Byrds in 1969
2. c. *Heartbreak Hotel*
3. c. *Wipe Out* / Surfaris
4. a. Ross Bagdasarian
5. c. Roy Orbison, with his hits *It's Over* and *Oh, Pretty Woman*
6. a. the Limeliters
7. b. 1926
8. c. musitron
9. a. Laurie
10. c. the Shirelles . . . Shirley Owens was better known later as Shirley Alston Reeves, and Doris Kenner as Doris Jackson
11. a. **Don Williams,** who was once a member of the Pozo–Seco Singers

****

Questions 12-16: SONG HITS

12. b. *Sweet Nothin's*
13. b. *Thou Shalt Not Steal*
14. b. *Quarter to Three*
15. b. *Goodbye Cruel World*
16. a. *Garden Party,* in 1972

****

Questions 17-20: HARDER QUESTIONS

17. c. the Supremes, a couple of years before Diana Ross (actually, Florence Ballard) selected the same name and took it to stardom
18. b. the Dreamlovers, who also charted with their own 1961 hit *When We Get Married*
19. b. Donny Osmond . . . Donny was the "seventh" son, but not the "seventh son of a seventh son" . . . Glen and Perry were !
20. c. one member's sister . . . the cover featured Jeff Barry, wife Ellie Greenwich, and Ellie's younger sister — pictured as such to appear as if they were a group and not merely a duo

Quiz 8

1. What is the only rock & roll single of the '60s that reached #1, fell off the charts, and then returned to reach #1 again ?

> a. *She Loves You* (Beatles)
>
> b. *The Twist* (Chubby Checker)
>
> c. *Monster Mash* (Bobby "Boris" Pickett)

****

2. Which of the following songs was originally written as a joke ?

> a. *Witch Doctor*
>
> b. *Teen Angel*
>
> c. *The Chipmunk Song*

****

3. Lesley Gore's hit *It's My Party* was released quickly because of news that another artist was scheduled to release the song. Who was this group ?

> a. the Murmaids
>
> b. Martha & the Vandellas
>
> c. the Crystals

****

4. What song was being referred to by the singer who said: "It sounded like hell, but the kids could dance to it."

> a. *Bristol Stomp*
>
> b. *The Twist*
>
> c. *Quarter to Three*

5. Who wrote the 1962 Clyde McPhatter hit *Lover Please*?

        a. Marvin Gaye

        b. Billy Swan

        c. Joe South

****

6. On which Elvis Presley ballad did someone in the studio drop a penny just as the song was concluding ?

        a. *Are You Lonesome Tonight*

        b. *Puppet on a String*

        c. *Love Me Tender*

****

7. What was the first #1 single recorded on the Epic record label ?

        a. *Roses Are Red* / Bobby Vinton

        b. *Over and Over* / Dave Clark Five

        c. *Washington Square* / Village Stompers

****

8. In what movie did the New Christy Minstrels 1964 hit *Today* appear ?

        a. *The Sweet Bird of Youth*

        b. *I'd Rather Be Rich*

        c. *Advance to the Rear*

9. What was the real (birth) name for singer Connie Francis ?

       a. Constance Ferragamo

       b. Concetta Franconero

       c. Connie Francis

****

10. Which group featured members including Cornelius, Fred, Ron and Gene ?

       a. the Contours

       b. the Five Satins

       c. the Marcels

****

11. On which label did Little Eva record her hit *The Loco-Motion* ?

       a. Dimension

       b. Garpax

       c. Monogram

****

Questions 12-16: SONG HITS

12. According to the Billboard Hot 100 singles chart, what was the most successful song for Mercury Records during the '50s & '60s ?

       a. *The Great Pretender*

       b. *Little Darlin'*

       c. *Running Bear*

13. Which of the following hits charted highest for Steve Lawrence on the U.S. Billboard singles chart ?

    a. *Pretty Blue Eyes*

    b. *Portrait Of My Love*

    c. *Go Away Little Girl*

****

14. What was Little Anthony & the Imperials' last U.S. Top 20 hit ?

    a. *Take Me Back*

    b. *Hurt So Bad*

    c. *I'm On The Outside (Looking In)*

****

15. What was Gene Chandler's first U.S. Billboard Top 40 hit ?

    a. *What Now*

    b. *Duke of Earl*

    c. *Bless Our Love*

****

16. Which of the following #1 hits charted the longest for Ray Charles on the U.S. Billboard singles chart ?

    a. *I Can't Stop Loving You*

    b. *Georgia On My Mind*

    c. *Hit the Road Jack*

HARDER QUESTIONS (17-20): 2 points each
(4 points if you can answer the question without the three choices !)

17. Who was the first Motown act to appear on Dick Clark's *American Bandstand* ?
      a. Mary Wells
      b. the Marvelettes
      c. the Miracles

****

18. Which of the following was NOT a former group name for the members of the Four Seasons ?
      a. the Valley Boys
      b. the Four Lovers
      c. the Variatones

****

19. Which group's members were resident dancers for Joey Dee & the Starliters at the Peppermint Lounge ?
      a. the Supremes
      b. the Angels
      c. the Ronettes

****

20. What unusual thing did Phil Spector do when recording the Ronettes in the studio ?
      a. he recorded them in total darkness
      b. he invited an audience to watch
      c. he decorated the studio with American flags

Quiz 8

1. b. *The Twist* (Chubby Checker) — #1 in 1960 and then again in 1961

2. b. *Teen Angel* ... The 1960 Mark Dinning hit was originally recorded to make fun of the tear-jerker so-called "death-rock" songs of the time ... but when a music publisher heard the humorous parody, he seriously liked it — and the rest is "death-rock history"

3. c. the Crystals

4. c. *Quarter to Three* ... the song was unintentionally recorded during an evening jam session with the group Daddy G., who had asked for Gary to ad lib some words to the instrumental *A Night With Daddy G* ... the result was a #1 hit in 1961

5. b. **Billy Swan,** singer of the 1974 hit *I Can Help*

6. a. *Are You Lonesome Tonight* (... listening closely, one can hear the penny drop just as the final chord is about to be played ...)

7. a. *Roses Are Red* / Bobby Vinton

8. c. *Advance to the Rear*

9. b. Concetta Franconero

10. c. the Marcels

11. a. Dimension

****

Questions 12-16: SONG HITS

12. b. *Little Darlin',* by the Diamonds

13. c. *Go Away Little Girl,* #1 for 2 weeks in 1963

14. a. *Take Me Back,* in 1965

15. b. *Duke of Earl*

16. a. *I Can't Stop Loving You,* #1 for 5 weeks in 1962

****

Questions 17-20: HARDER QUESTIONS

17. c. the Miracles

18. a. the Valley Boys

19. c. the Ronettes ... until Phil Spector signed them

20. a. he recorded them in total darkness so that lead singer Ronnie would not be distracted

Quiz 9

1. Who played piano on the Chiffons hit *He's So Fine* ?

      a. Petula Clark

      b. Billy Preston

      c. Carole King

****

2. Which father had a Top 20 hit after his daughter had a Top 20 hit ?

      a. Pat Boone

      b. Nat King Cole

      c. Rufus Thomas

****

3. What song did Chubby Checker imitate in 1965 ?

      a. *Do the Freddie*

      b. *The "In" Crowd*

      c. *The Name Game*

****

4. In 1964, Elvis sound–alike Terry Stafford scored with his hit *Suspicion,* but the song was actually recorded in 1962 by another rock star — who was it ?

      a. Roy Orbison

      b. Ral Donner

      c. Elvis Presley

5. Which legendary rock star's mother was a full-blooded Cherokee Indian ?

> a. Jerry Lee Lewis
> b. Ritchie Valens
> c. Jimi Hendrix

****

6. Who dueted with Big Dee Irwin in his 1963 hit *Swinging On a Star* ?

> a. Mary Wells
> b. Tina Turner
> c. Little Eva

****

7. Following the directions in Shirley Ellis' *The Name Game*, which of the following names would NOT be an "appropriate" name to select ?

> a. Bart
> b. Larry
> c. Will

****

8. What was Ronettes' lead singer Ronnie Spector's last name before she married Phil Spector ?

> a. Forrest
> b. Bennett
> c. LeMontaigne

9. What was the real (birth) name of Joey Dee ?

       a. Jeremy Vito–Lee

       b. Joseph Darin

       c. Joseph DiNicola

****

10. On which label did Little Anthony & the Imperials record their hits, including *Tears On My Pillow* ?

       a. End

       b. MGM

       c. Coed

****

11. Which '60s singer was born Eugene Dixon ?

       a. Gene McDaniels

       b. Gene Chandler

       c. Gene Pitney

****

Questions 12-16: SONG HITS

12. What was the Four Seasons' first single to reach the U.S. Billboard Top 20 record charts ?

       a. *Sherry*

       b. *Walk Like a Man*

       c. *Big Girls Don't Cry*

13. Which of the following hits charted highest for James Darren on the U.S. Billboard singles chart ?

a. *Goodbye Cruel World*

b. *Her Royal Majesty*

c. *Conscience*

****

14. What was Duane Eddy's last U.S. Top 40 hit ?

a. *The Ballad of Palladin*

b. *(Dance With the) Guitar Man*

c. *Boss Guitar*

****

15. What was the Shirelles' first U.S. #1 hit ?

a. *Soldier Boy*

b. *Will You Love Me Tomorrow*

c. *Mama Said*

****

16. What was Johnny Crawford's last U.S. Top 40 hit ?

a. *Proud*

b. *Your Nose Is Gonna Grow*

c. *Cindy's Birthday*

HARDER QUESTIONS (17-20): 2 points each
(4 points if you can answer the question without the three choices !)

17. Where did the '60s group the Essex first form ?

      a. during a talent show

      b. while in the military

      c. while attending college

****

18. What group did Freddy Cannon sing with before going solo ?

      a. the Cavaliers

      b. the Boomers

      c. the Spindrifts

****

19. What did the Trashmen call themselves before becoming notorious in 1964 for *Surfin' Bird (The Bird Is the Word)* ?

      a. the Citations

      b. the Hereafter

      c. Banzai

****

20. Which line in Shelley Fabares' *Johnny Angel* did sportscaster Bob Costas famously recite incorrectly in an interview in his show "Later With Bob Costas" ?

      a. "I'm in heaven — I get carried away."

      b. "I'd rather concentrate on Johnny Angel."

      c. "Together we will see how lovely heaven can be."

Quiz 9

1. c. **Carole King**
2. b. **Rufus Thomas** . . . his 1963 hit *Walkin' the Dog* came two years after his daughter Carla Thomas's hit *Gee Whiz (Look at His Eyes)*
3. a. *Do the Freddie* . . . his song *Let's Do the Freddie* barely reached the Top 40 chart, while Freddie & the Dreamers' *Do the Freddie* reached the Top 20 in 1965
4. c. **Elvis Presley**
5. c. **Jimi Hendrix**
6. c. **Little Eva**
7. a. **Bart** . . . Following the example "Nick," which goes: "Nick Nick, Bo-Bick, Banana Fanna Fo-Fick, Me My Mo-Mick", "Bart" would produce an unintended faux pas!
8. b. **Bennett**
9. c. **Joseph DiNicola**
10. a. **End**
11. b. **Gene Chandler**

****

Questions 12-16: SONG HITS

12. a. *Sherry,* in September, 1962
13. a. *Goodbye Cruel World,* reaching #3 in 1961
14. c. *Boss Guitar*
15. b. *Will You Love Me Tomorrow*
16. a. *Proud*

****

Questions 17-20: HARDER QUESTIONS

17. b. **while in the military** . . . they formed while in the Marine Corps, at Camp LeJeune
18. c. **the Spindrifts**
19. a. **the Citations**
20. b. **"I'd rather concentrate on Johnny Angel."** In his interview with Shelley Fabares, Costas proudly recalled the line "I'd rather contemplate on Johnny Angel" to which Fabares politely corrected him, leaving him speechless that "all these years" he'd remembered it wrong. It happens to all of us!

Quiz 10

1. Which group holds the record in the Rock era for the longest span between their first and last #1 U.S. Billboard single ?

    a. the Rolling Stones
    b. the Beach Boys
    c. the Beatles

****

2. Which famous singer played piano on the Shangri-Las' 1964 hit *Remember (Walkin' in the Sand)* ?

    a. Billy Joel
    b. Elton John
    c. Neil Sedaka

****

3. Which Top 10 Beach Boys hit was actually an adaptation of a Chuck Berry hit ?

    a. *Surfin' U.S.A.*
    b. *Barbara Ann*
    c. *Sloop John B*

****

4. What song was inspired by an incident in which Sonny Bono was barred admission to a restaurant due to his "mod" attire ?

    a. *The Beat Goes On*
    b. *Laugh At Me*
    c. *Little Man*

5. What was the Beatles first single-release in the U.S.?

>   a. *Love Me Do*
>   b. *From Me To You*
>   c. *I Want to Hold Your Hand*

****

6. On what 1965 Dick Clark show were Paul Revere & the Raiders the house band?

>   a. *Hullabaloo*
>   b. *Shindig*
>   c. *Where the Action Is*

****

7. Which rock group of the '60s had the most charted LPs during that decade?

>   a. the Ventures
>   b. the Beatles
>   c. the Beach Boys

****

8. Which song featured the lead singer stuttering?

>   a. *1-2-3* / Len Barry
>   b. *19th Nervous Breakdown* / Rolling Stones
>   c. *My Generation* / Who

9. On what television commercial did Robert Parker's *Barefootin'* appear ?

> a. Spic 'n' Span
>
> b. Mr. Clean
>
> c. Ajax

****

10. For what 1966 Peter Sellers movie did the Hollies record the theme ?

> a. *The Pink Panther*
>
> b. *Revenge of The Pink Panther*
>
> c. *After the Fox*

****

11. Which group was Dick Todd lead singer for ?

> a. the Standells
>
> b. Every Mother's Son
>
> c. the American Breed

****

12. Which group featured members including Don, Jim, Howard and Mark ?

> a. the Turtles
>
> b. the Soul Survivors
>
> c. the Electric Prunes

Questions 13-16: **SONG HITS**

****

13. What was Simon & Garfunkel's first single to reach the U.S. Billboard Top 20 record charts ?

　　　　　a. *Homeward Bound*

　　　　　b. *The Sounds of Silence*

　　　　　c. *I Am a Rock*

****

14. What was the Lettermen's last U.S. Top 40 hit ?

　　　　a. *Goin' Out of My Head/Can't Take My Eyes Off You*

　　　　b. *When I Fall In Love*

　　　　c. *Hurt So Bad*

****

15. Which of the following hits charted highest for the Lovin' Spoonful on the U.S. Billboard singles chart ?

　　　　a. *Do You Believe In Magic*

　　　　b. *Did You Ever Have to Make Up Your Mind*

　　　　c. *Summer In the City*

****

16. What was Ray Stevens' first U.S. Billboard Top 20 hit ?

　　　　　a. *Everything Is Beautiful*

　　　　　b. *Ahab, the Arab*

　　　　　c. *Gitarzan*

HARDER QUESTIONS (17-20): 2 points each
(4 points if you can answer the question without the three choices !)

17. Who did the Kinks begin as, prior to their more popular name ?
>>> a. the Beginners
>>> b. the Hedgehoppers
>>> c. the Ravens

****

18. Which of the following Seeds' singles was released first ?
>>> a. *Can't Seem to Make You Mine*
>>> b. *Pushin' Too Hard*
>>> c. *Mr. Farmer*

****

19. The Gentrys had a hit in 1965 with *Keep on Dancing.* Which group had earlier released the song, in 1963 ?
>>> a. the Avantis
>>> b. the Rajas
>>> c. the Barrons

****

20. What was the name of the very first singer the Beatles served as a backup group for ?
>>> a. Wally
>>> b. Tony
>>> c. Rory

Quiz 10

1. b. **the Beach Boys** ... 24 years, from 1964's *I Get Around* to 1988's *Kokomo*
2. a. **Billy Joel**
3. b. *Surfin' U.S.A.,* adapted from Chuck Berry's *Sweet Little Sixteen*
4. b. *Laugh At Me,* in what Cher described as an emotional reaction to the couple's humiliating event
5. b. *From Me To You* . . . it was not a hit, however, not even reaching the Hot 100 . . . as a side note, *Love Me Do* was their first single-release in England, in 1962, reaching America two years later — and then it returned to the Top 10 in England 20 years later, in 1982!
6. c. *Where the Action Is*
7. c. **the Beach Boys**
8. c. *My Generation* / Who
9. a. **Spic 'n' Span**
10. c. *After the Fox*
11. a. **the Standells**
12. a. **the Turtles**

****

Questions 13-16: SONG HITS

13. b. *The Sounds of Silence,* in 1965
14. c. *Hurt So Bad*
15. c. *Summer In the City,* #1 for 3 weeks in 1966
16. b. *Ahab, the Arab,* in 1962

****

Questions 17-20: HARDER QUESTIONS

17. c. **the Ravens**
18. a. *Can't Seem to Make You Mine,* shortly before *Pushin' Too Hard,* in 1965 ... *Mr. Farmer* was released two years later, in 1967 ... soon thereafter, a reissue of *Pushin' Too Hard* in 1967 became the group's first and only single to crack the Billboard Top 40, which was then followed by the re-release of *Can't Seem to Make You Mine*
19. a. **the Avantis**
20. a. **Wally** . . . In 1960, the Beatles recorded *Summertime* and *Fever* on an acetate 78rm record — the singer, Wally, was from another well-known Liverpool group, Rory Storm & the Hurricanes . . . the Hurricane's drummer, Ringo Starr, played in place of Beatles drummer Pete Best on the tracks

Quiz 11

1. How many people saw the Beatles first gig in Aldershot, England, in 1961?
   - a. 18
   - b. 157
   - c. 14,500

****

2. Who first suggested the group name "Beach Boys" ?
   - a. the Wilsons' mother
   - b. the group's publicist
   - c. a group member

****

3. On what show did the Byrds make their TV network debut ?
   - a. *Shindig*
   - b. *Hullabaloo*
   - c. *The Ed Sullivan Show*

****

4. What is the only hit song Herman's Hermits recorded in America ?
   - a. *Mrs. Brown You've Got a Lovely Daughter*
   - b. *I'm Henry VIII I Am*
   - c. *A Must to Avoid*

5. What did listeners — especially radio deejays — think about the Righteous Brothers' 1965 iconic hit *You've Lost That Lovin' Feelin'* upon first hearing the opening line ?

    a. that it was another group singing the song

    b. that the background instrumental track had accidentally been omitted

    c. that it was on the wrong speed

****

6. What was the original name of Gerry Marsden's group before being known as Gerry & the Pacemakers ?

    a. Mars & the Planets

    b. the Mars Bars

    c. the Liverpool Exports

****

7. Under which of the following names did Sonny Bono NOT once record ?

    a. Don Christy

    b. Julian Turner

    c. Ronny Sommers

****

8. Which surf band was Ritchie Burns the leader of ?

    a. the Rivieras

    b. the Rip Chords

    c. the Hondells

9. How many Billboard #1 hits did the Beatles have in the United Kingdom during the '60s ?

        a. 17

        b. 21

        c. 34

****

10. According to the Billboard Hot 100 singles chart, what was the most successful song for Uni Records during the '60s ?

        a. *Incense and Peppermints*

        b. *Sweet Caroline*

        c. *Build Me Up Buttercup*

****

11. John Phillips and Scott McKenzie were both members of which group ?

        a. the Mamas & the Papas

        b. the Mugwumps

        c. the Journeymen

****

12. What '60s/'70s singer was born Leonard Ainsworth ?

        a. Brook Benton

        b. Dobie Gray

        c. Neil Diamond

Questions 13-16: SONG HITS

****

13. Which of the following #1 hits charted for the longest for Simon & Garfunkel on the U.S. Billboard singles chart ?

    a. *The Sounds of Silence*

    b. *Mrs. Robinson*

    c. *Bridge Over Troubled Water*

****

14. What was Sonny & Cher's first single to reach the U.S. Billboard Top 20 record charts ?

    a. *Baby Don't Go*

    b. *I Got You Babe*

    c. *The Beat Goes On*

****

15. What was the Box Tops' only U.S. #1 hit ?

    a. *Cry Like a Baby*

    b. *Choo Choo Train*

    c. *The Letter*

****

16. What was the Beatles' first single to reach the U.S. Billboard Top 20 record charts ?

    a. *I Want To Hold Your Hand*

    b. *She Loves You*

    c. *Twist and Shout*

HARDER QUESTIONS (17-20): 2 points each
(4 points if you can answer the question without the three choices !)

17. Which group was being referred to as "a nightmare — musically they are a near disaster . . . guitars and drums slamming out a merciless beat that does away with secondary rhythms . . . their lyrics are a catastrophe . . . of valentine-card sentiments."
> a. the Beatles
> b. the Troggs
> c. the Rolling Stones

****

18. On what television show did the Rolling Stones make their U.S. debut appearance ?
> a. *The Les Crane Show*
> b. *The Tonight Show*
> c. *The Ed Sullivan Show*

****

19. What were Mitch Ryder and the Detriot Wheels originally known as ?
> a. the Memphis Experiment
> b. Billy Lee & the Rivieras
> c. the Manhattan Dimension

****

20. Who was the *first* drummer that John Lennon, in his earliest rehearsals, collaborated with ?
> a. Tommy Moore
> b. Norman Chapman
> c. Colin Hanton

Quiz 11

1. a. 18
2. b. the group's publicist, a promotions man from their first label, Candix
3. b. *Hullabaloo,* in May, 1965
4. c. *A Must to Avoid,* which was recorded during the filming of MGM's *Hold On!*
5. c. that it was on the wrong speed . . . Bill Medley's voice was so low on the opening line "you never close your eyes anymore when I kiss your lips" that many thought the 45 rpm record was actually being played at 33⅓ rpm !
6. b. the Mars Bars . . . his intent was to gain sponsorship from the candy-maker — instead, he was threatened with a lawsuit and quickly changed the name
7. b. Julian Turner
8. c. the Hondells
9. a. 17
10. a. *Incense and Peppermints,* by the Strawberry Alarm Clock
11. c. the Journeymen
12. b. Dobie Gray

****

Questions 13-16: **SONG HITS**

13. c. *Bridge Over Troubled Water,* #1 for 6 weeks in 1970
14. b. *I Got You Babe,* in August, 1965
15. c. *The Letter*
16. a. *I Want To Hold Your Hand,* in January, 1964

****

Questions 17-20: **HARDER QUESTIONS**

17. a. the Beatles, from a 1964 *Newsweek* cover-story on the Beatles
18. a. *The Les Crane Show,* on June 2, 1964
19. b. Billy Lee & the Rivieras
20. c. Colin Hanton, according to John's sister, who would watch them practice in her family's kitchen, Colin banging on a tea chest rather than a drum as John played his earliest compositions . . . Hanton later played with the Quarrymen

Quiz 12

1. The Rolling Stones' name was taken from a Muddy Waters song. Who first suggested the name ?
   - a. Muddy Waters
   - b. Brian Jones
   - c. John Lennon

****

2. Who recorded the 1964 Beatles-tribute record *Ringo, I Love You* ?
   - a. Petula Clark
   - b. Lesley Gore
   - c. Cher

****

3. From what book did the Doors get their group's name ?
   - a. *The Doors of Perception*
   - b. *Unlocking the Doors of the Imagination*
   - c. *Through the Doors of Time*

****

4. Who wrote *Different Drum*, the Stone Poneys' biggest hit ?
   - a. Kenny Rogers
   - b. Michael Nesmith
   - c. Linda Ronstadt

5. Which rock festival featured groups such as the Byrds, the Association, the Who, Jimi Hendrix and the Grateful Dead ?

> a. the Newport Pop Festival
> b. the Monterey Pop Festival
> c. Woodstock

****

6. Who sang lead on the Beach Boys #1 hit *Help Me Rhonda* ?

> a. Carl Wilson
> b. Al Jardine
> c. Dennis Wilson

****

7. At what famous British club in Liverpool did the Beatles make their debut ?

> a. the Casbah Club
> b. the Star-Club
> c. the Cavern Club

****

8. What famous street corner is associated with the earliest days of the Jefferson Airplane ?

> a. Hollywood and Vine
> b. Haight and Ashbury
> c. Beverly and Wilshire

9. Just before Jan Berry crashed his Corvette and was nearly killed, what news had he received ?

    a. that he was soon to be drafted

    b. that he was accepted into U.C.L.A.

    c. that his mom had kicked him out of the house

****

10. Which group featured members including Otis, Paul, David and Eddie ?

    a. the Young Rascals

    b. the Newbeats

    c. the Temptations

****

11. What was the real (birth) name of Troggs leader Reg Presley ?

    a. Reginald Ball

    b. Ranford Smythe

    c. Preston Reginald

****

12. On which label did Sonny & Cher record their hits, including *I Got You Babe* ?

    a. Atco

    b. Decca

    c. Mirwood

Questions 13-16: SONG HITS

****

13. Which of the following hits charted highest for Jan & Dean on the U.S. Billboard singles chart ?

      a. *Surf City*

      b. *Dead Man's Curve*

      c. *The Little Old Lady From Pasadena*

****

14. What was Roger Miller's last U.S. Top 20 hit ?

      a. *Engine Engine #9*

      b. *King of the Road*

      c. *England Swings*

****

15. Which song was the only #1 U.S. hit single for the Dave Clark Five ?

      a. *Over & Over*

      b. *Because*

      c. *Glad All Over*

****

16. What was the Who's first U.S. Billboard Top 40 hit ?

      a. *My Generation*

      b. *Happy Jack*

      c. *I Can See For Miles*

17. Which of the following was NOT a name the Hollies used before their climb to music fame ?

> a. the Deltas
>
> b. the Fortunes
>
> c. the Chippers

****

18. On what '60s instrumental hit did Walker Brother member Scott Engel play electric bass guitar ?

> a. *Telstar*
>
> b. *Walk Don't Run*
>
> c. *Let's Go*

****

19. After the success of *Help!* and *A Hard Days Night,* the Beatles planned a third movie, which was never made. What was the proposed title for the movie ?

> a. *A Talent for Loving*
>
> b. *Over the Edge*
>
> c. *Strawberry Fields Forever*

****

20. What group was referred to in a 1961 British *Mersey Beat* magazine issue, calling the Liverpool group "beyond comparison . . . in a class by themselves" ?

> a. the Searchers
>
> b. the Swinging Blue Jeans
>
> c. the Beatles

Quiz 12

1. b. Brian Jones
2. c. Cher (billed as Bonnie Jo Mason)
3. a. *The Doors of Perception,* Aldous Huxley's book, in which "doors" are equated with drugs . . . sources also attribute the name to a passage from 18th century poet William Blake: "There are things that are known and things that are unknown; in between are doors" . . .
4. b. Michael Nesmith (Monkees)
5. b. the 1967 Monterey Pop Festival
6. b. Al Jardine
7. c. the Cavern Club, as the Quarrymen . . . Paul McCartney had not yet joined and did not perform at the debut
8. b. Haight and Ashbury
9. a. that he was soon to be drafted
10. c. the Temptations
11. a. Reginald Ball
12. a. Atco

****

Questions 13-16: SONG HITS

13. a. *Surf City,* #1 for 2 weeks in 1963
14. c. *England Swings*
15. a. *Over & Over,* in 1965
16. b. *Happy Jack* . . . strange though it may seem, *My Generation* never cracked the Top 40 !

****

Questions 17-20: HARDER QUESTIONS

17. c. the Chippers
18. c. *Let's Go,* as a member of the 1963 group, the Routers
19. a. *A Talent for Loving,* the book upon which it was to be based
20. b. the Swinging Blue Jeans . . . in fact, in a poll of competing bands, the magazine took the Swinging Blue Jeans out of the race because of their "superior" talent . . . without them in the running, the Beatles won the poll

Quiz 13

1. Johnny Maestro, lead singer of the early '60s group the Crests, formed which late '60s group ?

 a. Friend and Lover

 b. Spiral Staircase

 c. the Brooklyn Bridge

****

2. Who wrote the Vogues' 1965 hit *You're the One* ?

 a. Sonny Bono

 b. Petula Clark

 c. Tom Jones

****

3. Which well-known manager signed Billy J. Kramer & the Dakotas to a multi-year contract ?

 a. Tony Hatch

 b. Andrew Loog Oldham

 c. Brian Epstein

****

4. In what '60s movie did Wayne Fontana & the Mindbenders appear ?

 a. *Alfie*

 b. *Blow Up*

 c. *To Sir With Love*

5. Although popular in the U.K. long before the Hollies broke into the U.S. charts, what song finally launched their success in the states ?

  a. *Bus Stop*
  b. *Carrie-Ann*
  c. *Look Through Any Window*

****

6. What event in Bob Dylan's life changed his musical style, leading to a more introspective and simple, often religious, focus ?

  a. a motorcycle accident
  b. a bitter divorce
  c. first hearing the Beatles *Nowhere Man*

****

7. In what now-historic 1965 concert did the Young Rascals play ?

  a. Altamont
  b. the Newport Folk Festival
  c. Shea Stadium

****

8. Who of the following was NOT a guitarist at one time for the Yardbirds ?

  a. Pete Townshend
  b. Eric Clapton
  c. Jimmy Page

9. In what year was Tommy James & the Shondells'
1965 hit Hanky Panky first recorded ?
>   a. 1960
>
>   b. 1963
>
>   c. 1965

****

10. Which group was Bucky Wilkin the leader of ?
>   a. the Beau Brummels
>
>   b. the Strangeloves
>
>   c. Ronny & the Daytonas

****

11. On which label did the Hollies record their hits,
including *Stop! Stop! Stop!* ?
>   a. Epic
>
>   b. Imperial
>
>   c. Atlantic

****

12. What was the real (birth) name of the lead singer
of Spanky & Our Gang ?
>   a. Elaine McFarlane
>
>   b. Susan Littlefield
>
>   c. Sandy Fiorina

Questions 13-16: **SONG HITS**

****

13. What was Herman's Hermits' last U.S. Top 40 hit ?

    a. *Museum*

    b. *I Can Take Or Leave Your Loving*

    c. *Don't Go Out Into the Rain (You're Going to Melt)*

****

14. What was Neil Diamond's first million-selling single ?

    a. *Sweet Caroline*

    b. *Cherry Cherry*

    c. *Kentucky Woman*

****

15. Which of the following hits charted highest for Mitch Ryder & the Detroit Wheels on the U.S. Billboard singles chart ?

    a. *Jenny Take a Ride*

    b. *Devil With a Blue Dress On/Good Golly Miss Molly*

    c. *Sock It To Me, Baby!*

****

16. What was Sonny & Cher's last U.S. Top 20 hit ?

    a. *All I Ever Need Is You*

    b. *A Cowboy's Work Is Never Done*

    c. *Little Man*

17. What group was known as Memphis's "blue-eyed soul" answer to New York's Young Rascals ?
      a. the Box Tops
      b. the Righteous Brothers
      c. the American Breed

****

18. Which of the following groups was formed to raise money to help their soccer team travel to Holland for a match ?
      a. the Hollies
      b. Herman's Hermits
      c. the Dave Clark Five

****

19. What was a former name for Paul Revere & the Raiders ?
      a. the Starfires
      b. the Downbeats
      c. the Backstreet Five

****

20. Which musician joined the pre-Beatles band Johnny & the Moondogs as they toured, being the first to suggest a new group name, the Silver Beetles ?
      a. Pete Best
      b. Rory Storm
      c. Stu Sutcliffe

Quiz 13

1. c. the Brooklyn Bridge, whose hit *Worst That Could Happen* reached #3 in 1969
2. b. Petula Clark
3. c. Brian Epstein, manager of the Beatles
4. c. *To Sir With Love*
5. a. *Bus Stop* . . . though *Look Through Any Window* was their first release that broke into the U.S. charts, it was nowhere near "hit" status
6. a. a motorcycle accident in 1966
7. c. Shea Stadium, as an opening act for the Beatles' New York sellout
8. a. Pete Townshend
9. a. In 1960, when only 12 years old, Tommy James formed a group called the Shondells, who played for school dances. It was at that time they recorded and released *Hanky Panky* on a local record label . . . Five years later, a disc jockey found a copy and played it on the air, attracting interest from Roulette Records executives, who purchased the rights to the record . . . Because the original group had long since disbanded, Tommy James had to find a new set of Shondells after the song suddenly and unexpectedly topped the charts in 1966!
10. c. Ronny & the Daytonas
11. b. Imperial
12. a. Elaine McFarlane

****

Questions 13-16: SONG HITS
13. b. *I Can Take Or Leave Your Loving,* in 1968
14. a. *Sweet Caroline*
15. b. *Devil With a Blue Dress On/Good Golly Miss Molly,* reaching #4 in 1966
16. b. *A Cowboy's Work Is Never Done*

****

Questions 17-20: HARDER QUESTIONS
17. a. the Box Tops
18. c. the Dave Clark Five
19. b. the Downbeats, who recorded the instrumental *Like, Long Hair* in 1961
20. c. Stu Sutcliffe

Quiz 14

1. Who did Paul McCartney originally offer his song *A World Without Love* to, prior to the successful recording by Peter & Gordon ?

   a. the Searchers

   b. the Dave Clark Five

   c. Billy J. Kramer & the Dakotas

****

2. What did Marvin Gaye once want to become ?

   a. a professional football player

   b. a dance choreographer

   c. a professional boxer

****

3. Under what name did the Animals first record ?

   a. the Alan Price Combo

   b. the Newcastle Knights

   c. the Wild Cats

****

4. What inspired Tommy James to call his band "the Shondells" ?

   a. a movie

   b. a childhood sweetheart

   c. a singer

5. Why did the Byrds select the unusual spelling for their name ?

a. to poke fun at the movie *Bye Bye Birdie*

b. so as not to be confused with "birds," a British slang for "girls"

c. to express their allegiance to Bob Dylan

****

6. Which of the two members of the teen-trio Dino, Desi & Billy did NOT have at least one famous entertainment parent ?

a. Dino

b. Desi

c. Billy

****

7. What was the first Lennon/McCartney non-Beatles song to reach #1 on the U.S. singles chart ?

a. *Bad to Me* (Billy J. Kramer & the Dakotas)

b. *A World Without Love* (Peter & Gordon)

c. *Needles and Pins* (Searchers)

****

8. What was the name of the 1966 Johnny Rivers hit which originally came from a British weekly television show ?

a. *Secret Asian Man*

b. *Secret Aging Man*

c. *Secret Agent Man*

9. Warner Brothers purchased Valiant Records in 1967 primarily to acquire the recording rights of what group ?

> a. the Association
>
> b. the Ides of March
>
> c. Peter, Paul & Mary

****

10. Who was the lead singer for Paul Revere & the Raiders ?

> a. Paul Revere
>
> b. Freddie Weller
>
> c. Mark Lindsay

****

11. Which group featured members including Gary, Bill, Danny and Alex ?

> a. the Music Explosion
>
> b. the Soul Survivors
>
> c. the Box Tops

****

12. In what movie did *Ticket to Ride* appear ?

> a. *Help!*
>
> b. *A Hard Day's Night*
>
> c. *Let It Be*

Questions 13-16: **SONG HITS**

****

13. What was Marvin Gaye's first single to reach the U.S. Billboard Top 20 record charts ?

        a. *You're a Wonderful One*

        b. *Pride and Joy*

        c. *Ain't That Peculiar*

****

14. What was the Monkees' last U.S. Top 20 single of the '60s ?

        a. *Valleri*

        b. *D. W. Washburn*

        c. *Words*

****

15. What was Tommy Roe's first U.S. Billboard Top 40 hit ?

        a. *Sheila*

        b. *Everybody*

        c. *Sweet Pea*

****

16. Which of the following hits charted highest for Wilson Pickett on the U.S. Billboard singles chart ?

        a. *In the Midnight Hour*

        b. *Land of 1000 Dances*

        c. *Funky Broadway*

17. Which Beatles hit stayed on the Hot 100 U.S. Billboard singles chart for the most weeks ?

   a. *Can't Buy Me Love*

   b. *Hey Jude*

   c. *Twist and Shout*

****

18. Under which of the following names did one of the Young Rascals once record ?

   a. Felix & the Escorts

   b. Dino & the Delegates

   c. Eddie & the Hot Rods

****

19. Along with temporary membership as a Beach Boy, what early '60s instrumental group was Glen Campbell also a member ?

   a. the Champs

   b. the Surfaris

   c. the Ventures

****

20. Who said the following: "I enjoy performing other people's songs. I'm not a musician. When I hear a song that I like, I sing it as a part that myself as an actor can play — that's basically what I am: an actor but on the rock and roll stage."

   a. Roger Daltry

   b. Eric Burdon

   c. Davy Jones

Quiz 14

1. c. Billy J. Kramer & the Dakotas, but they respectfully declined
2. a. a professional football player . . . he tried out for the Detroit Lions
3. a. the Alan Price Combo . . . Alan Price was keyboardist for the original Animals
4. c. a singer . . . he named his band after singer Troy Shondell, who had a Top 10 hit in 1961 with *This Time*
5. b. so as not to be confused with "birds," a British slang for "girls"
6. c. Billy . . . Dino's dad was Dean Martin; Desi's parents were Desi Arnaz and Lucille Ball
7. b. *A World Without Love* (Peter & Gordon)
8. c. *Secret Agent Man* (originally composed for the TV series *Danger Man*, which ran from 1964–1966)
9. a. the Association
10. c. Mark Lindsay . . . Paul Revere was the keyboardist
11. c. the Box Tops
12. a. *Help!*

****

Questions 13-16: SONG HITS

13. b. *Pride and Joy,* in 1963
14. b. *D. W. Washburn . . .That Was Then, This Is Now,* which featured original Monkees Micky Dolenz and Peter Tork, reached #20 in 1986
15. a. *Sheila*
16. b. *Land of 1000 Dances,* reaching #6 in 1966

****

Questions 17-20: HARDER QUESTIONS

17. c. *Twist and Shout* . . . 26 weeks total: spending 11 weeks in 1964 and 15 weeks in 1966; *Hey Jude* was on the Hot 100 singles chart for 19 weeks
18. a. Felix & the Escorts, a band which also included Neil Diamond
19. a. the Champs, but long after their #1 hit *Tequila*
20. b. Eric Burdon

Quiz 15

1. What prompted the Byrds to write and sing *Eight Miles High* ?
   - a. a drug experience aboard a plane
   - b. a recent trip to England
   - c. the Beatles song *Eight Days a Week*

****

2. Where did the Beatles record their first album ?
   - a. at Abbey Road Studios
   - b. at EMI Studios
   - c. in a local Liverpool recording studio

****

3. In what U.S. movie did Herman's Hermits make a cameo appearance while first visiting the states ?
   - a. *Freakout U.S.A.*
   - b. *When the Boys Meet the Girls*
   - c. *Bikini Beach Party*

****

4. Who commented, on the death of a close compatriot, that the group was "finished when [he] died. I knew, deep inside me, that that was it. Without him, we'd had it." ?
   - a. Mick Jagger, regarding fellow Rolling Stone, Brian Jones
   - b. Jeff Beck, regarding Yardbirds lead singer, Keith Relf
   - c. John Lennon, regarding manager Brian Epstein

5. Which of the following groups did NOT dress up in Colonial attire ?

> a. the Young Rascals
>
> b. Paul Revere & the Raiders
>
> c. the New Colony Six

****

6. What did Righteous Brothers Bobby Hatfield once try out for ?

> a. a part in a Broadway musical
>
> b. a spot on a professional baseball team
>
> c. a role as one of the Monkees

****

7. Why were many radio stations hesitant to play the 1967 Soul Survivors hit *Expressway to Your Heart* ?

> a. it contained distracting noises
>
> b. it contained an objectional lyric
>
> c. it was deemed too long for AM airplay

****

8. Which of the following hits from 1967 does NOT contain the words of the title in its lyrics ?

a. *The Happening* / Supremes

b. *Gimme Little Sign* / Brenton Wood

c. *Him Or Me — What's It Gonna Be* / Paul Revere & the Raiders

9. Which of the following singers was stricken with polio as a young girl ?

> a. Petula Clark
>
> b. Judy Collins
>
> c. Connie Francis

****

10. On which label did Johnny Rivers record his hits, including *Secret Agent Man* ?

> a. Columbia
>
> b. Epic
>
> c. Imperial

****

11. In which movie did the Seeds and Strawberry Alarm Clock appear ?

> a. *Wild In the Streets*
>
> b. *Psychout*
>
> c. *The Savage Seven*

****

12. Which group featured members including Robert, Terry, James and Peter ?

> a. Chicago
>
> b. the Association
>
> c. the Tremeloes

Questions 13-16: SONG HITS

****

13. What was the Four Tops' first single to reach the U.S. Billboard Top 20 record charts ?

       a. *Baby I Need Your Loving*

       b. *I Can't Help Myself*

       c. *Reach Out I'll Be There*

****

14. What was the Dave Clark Five's last U.S. Top 20 hit ?

       a. *You Got What It Takes*

       b. *At the Scene*

       c. *Try Too Hard*

****

15. What was Spanky & Our Gang's first U.S. Billboard Top 40 hit ?

       a. *Lazy Day*

       b. *Like to Get to Know You*

       c. *Sunday Will Never Be the Same*

****

16. Which of the following hits charted highest for Gary Lewis & the Playboys on the U.S. Billboard singles chart ?

       a. *This Diamond Ring*

       b. *Count Me In*

       c. *Save Your Heart For Me*

17. The Omens, singing as the Beach Bums, recorded a parody of Ssgt. Barry Sadler's *The Ballad of the Green Berets,* entitled *The Ballad of the Yellow Beret* under the "Are You Kidding Me?" label. Although a popular local hit, the record was quickly withdrawn after Sadler threatened a lawsuit. Who co-wrote and sang on this 1966 novelty record ?

    a. Barry McGuire

    b. Tommy James

    c. Bob Seger

****

18. What was a former name for the American Breed ?

    a. Made in America

    b. the Silent Majority

    c. Gary & the Nitelites

****

19. What early group consisted of "Mama" Cass Elliott, "Papa" Denny Dougherty, and *Hey Joe'*s Tim Rose ?

    a. the Mugwumps

    b. the Beefeaters

    c. the Big Three

****

20. From where was the Beatles second *Ed Sullivan Show* appearance recorded ?

    a. NBC Sound Studios #1 and #2

    b. the Waldorf-Astoria Hotel

    c. the Deauville Hotel

Quiz 15

1. b. a recent trip to England . . . The song was a reflection of the "rain grey town" and of the street signs that don't really guide you, a land that is stranger than it is known. Needless to say, the Byrds' arrival was not well-received by the Britishers either, most of whom unjustly felt the American group a threat to the British Merseybeat dominance . . . Several venues were cancelled due to low ticket-sales, and the song itself failed to perform well in the U.S.A. — due to another false-association that it was drug-related.

2. a. at Abbey Road Studios, London, in 1963

3. b. *When the Boys Meet the Girls*

4. c. John Lennon, regarding manager Brian Epstein

5. a. the Young Rascals, who at one time dressed up wearing Knickerbockers

6. b. a spot on the Los Angeles Dodgers baseball team

7. a. it contained distracting noises . . . specifically, the song included real car horns, which radio stations felt could cause automobile listeners to think the honking was actually taking place on the road

8. b. *Gimme Little Sign* / Brenton Wood . . .the lyrics are "Just give me some kind of sign, girl"

9. b. Judy Collins, successfully recovering by age twelve

10. c. Imperial

11. b. *Psychout*

12. a. Chicago

****

Questions 13-16: SONG HITS

13. a. *Baby I Need Your Loving,* in 1964

14. a. *You Got What It Takes*

15. c. *Sunday Will Never Be the Same*

16. a. *This Diamond Ring,* #1 for 2 weeks in 1965

****

Questions 17-20: HARDER QUESTIONS

17. c. Bob Seger

18. c. Gary & the Nitelites

19. c. the Big Three

20. c. Miami's Deauville Hotel

Quiz 16

1. What was the #1 single of 1965 ?

    a. *Yesterday*

    b. *(I Can't Get No) Satisfaction*

    c. *Wooly Bully*

****

2. Which album inspired Beach Boys leader Brian Wilson to create his epic LP *Pet Sounds* ?

    a. *Rubber Soul*

    b. *The Sounds of Silence*

    c. *Ferry Across the Mersey*

****

3. Which of the following historical figures was removed from the final cover of the Beatles' *Sgt. Pepper's Lonely Hearts Club Band* LP cover ?

    a. Mahatma Gandhi

    b. Jesus Christ

    c. Buddha

****

4. What is another name that 1969 *Cinnamon* singer Derek was known by ?

    a. Johnny Cymbal

    b. David Seville

    c. Dickey Lee

5. Which group did Paul Pond, who was in an early '60s band with Brian Jones, later become lead singer for ?

        a. Vanilla Fudge

        b. the Grass Roots

        c. Manfred Mann

****

6. What spin-off record label did Johnny Rivers launch in 1966 ?

        a. Valiant

        b. Bang

        c. Soul City

****

7. What Beatles song did American songwriter Jerry Leiber reportedly say was the best song ever written ?

        a. *Eleanor Rigby*

        b. *A Day in the Life*

        c. *Revolution*

****

8. What was the first song released in which the members of the Monkees actually played their own instruments ?

        a. *Words*

        b. *Take a Giant Step*

        c. *The Girl I Knew Somewhere*

9. Before he achieved fame in the music world with Buffalo Springfield, what did Neil Young drive ?

  a. a tractor

  b. a hearse

  c. a vintage Model–T Ford

****

10. Which group featured members including Joe, Steve and John ?

  a. the Surfaris

  b. the Lovin' Spoonful

  c. the Animals

****

11. On which label did Petula Clark record her hits, including *Downtown* ?

  a. Parrot

  b. Warner Brothers

  c. Capitol

****

12. The 1968 Max Frost & the Troopers hit *Nothing Can Change the Shape of Things to Come* was the theme song for what movie ?

  a. *The Wild Angels*

  b. *Wild in the Streets*

  c. *The Wild Bunch*

Questions 13-16: SONG HITS

****

13. What was the Young Rascals' first single to reach the U.S. Billboard Top 20 record charts ?

      a. *Good Lovin'*

      b. *Groovin'*

      c. *A Beautiful Morning*

****

14. Which of the following hits charted highest for Steppenwolf on the U.S. Billboard singles chart ?

      a. *Rock Me*

      b. *Born to Be Wild*

      c. *Magic Carpet Ride*

****

15. What was Billy Joe Royal's first U.S. Billboard Top 40 hit ?

      a. *I Knew You When*

      b. *Cherry Hill Park*

      c. *Down In the Boondocks*

****

16. What was the Turtles' last U.S. Top 40 hit ?

      a. *Elenore*

      b. *You Showed Me*

      c. *She's My Girl*

HARDER QUESTIONS (17-20): 2 points each
(4 points if you can answer the question without the three choices !)

17. On what television commercial did the Beach Boys' *California Girls* appear ?

    a. Clairol Herbal Essence

    b. Stridex Medicated Pads

    c. Ray-Ban Sunglasses

****

18. What was the original name of leader Arthur Lee's Los Angeles band, Love ?

    a. Peace and Happiness

    b. the Overnight Dew

    c. the Grass Roots

****

19. Snuff Garrett reportedly remarked that Cher's *Gypsies, Tramps & Thieves* was one of the two favorite records that he produced. What was the other record ?

    a. *Old Rivers* / Walter Brennan

    b. *Big Bad John* / Jimmy Dean

    c. *Everybody Loves a Clown* / Gary Lewis & the Playboys

****

20. On what program did the Beatles unveil their 1967 worldwide live performance of *All You Need Is Love* ?

    a. the "Cosmic Events" global presentation

    b. the "Capitol Extravaganza" international concert

    c. the "Our World" global show

Quiz 16

1. c. *Wooly Bully,* by Sam the Sham & the Pharaohs
2. a. *Rubber Soul,* the Beatles' #1 album
3. b. Jesus Christ . . . though originally intended for inclusion, it was taken off the cover following John Lennon's "greater than Jesus" scandal
4. a. Johnny Cymbal, whose 1963 single *Mr. Bass Man* was a Top 20 hit
5. c. Manfred Mann, singing as Paul Jones
6. c. Soul City Records, which later featured groups such as the 5th Dimension
7. a. *Eleanor Rigby*
8. c. *The Girl I Knew Somewhere*
9. b. a hearse
10. b. the Lovin' Spoonful, with Zal, too
11. b. Warner Brothers
12. b. *Wild in the Streets,* starring Christopher Jones

****

Questions 13-16: SONG HITS

13. a. *Good Lovin',* in 1966
14. b. *Born to Be Wild,* #2 in 1968
15. c. *Down In the Boondocks*
16. b. *You Showed Me*

****

Questions 17-20: HARDER QUESTIONS

17. a. Clairol Herbal Essence
18. c. the Grass Roots, soon changed to avoid conflict with the other Los Angeles band called the Grass Roots, a group that was soon to become a nationwide supergroup
19. a. *Old Rivers* / Walter Brennan, a spoken-word story song from 1962
20. c. the "Our World" global show

Quiz 17

1. Which of the following drummers was NOT a Mousketeer earlier in his life ?
             a. Cubby O'Brien
             b. Johnny Cowsill
             c. Dick Dodd

****

2. Which of the following songs does NOT contain the title in the lyrics ?
             a. *Tighten Up* (Archie Bell & the Drells)
             b. *Mony Mony* (Tommy James & the Shondells)
             c. *Reach Out of the Darkness* (Friend & Lover)

****

3. What did Jimi Hendrix do during the 1967 Monterey Pop Festival performance that singled him out as a truly unique audience-pleaser ?
             a. he set his guitar on fire
             b. he invited four spectators to join him on stage
             c. he played his electric guitar with his toes

****

4. Who was once referred to as the British Dylan ?
             a. Rod Stewart
             b. Noel Harrison
             c. Donovan

5. Although the lawsuit was later dropped, the copyright holders of what song claimed that Creedence Clearwater Revival's hit *Travelin' Band* plagiarized their tune ?

    a. *Travelin' Man*

    b. *Purple People Eater*

    c. *Good Golly Miss Molly*

****

6. Which song did Dr. Timothy Leary reportedly wish to use as his campaign song when he ran for California governor in 1969 ?

    a. *Good Vibrations*

    b. *Get Together*

    c. *Come Together*

****

7. Beatle George Harrison performed a guitar lick on Cream's *Badge.* On what Beatles song did Eric Clapton, returning the favor, play lead guitar ?

    a. *Nowhere Man*

    b. *Here Comes the Sun*

    c. *While My Guitar Gently Weeps*

****

8. In what year was the original version of Johnny Cash's *Folsum Prison Blues* released, a live version of which reached the Top 40 in 1968 ?

    a. 1956

    b. 1960

    c. 1967

9. Who sang lead in the Supremes hits *Up the Ladder to the Roof, Stoned Love* and *Nathan Jones* ?

  a. Cindy Birdsong

  b. Jean Terrell

  c. Diana Ross

****

10. What was Mitch Ryder's real (birth) name ?

  a. William Levise, Jr.

  b. Conrad Mitchell Rydell

  c. Mitchell Ryder Bernstein

****

11. What movie did Frank Sinatra's 1966 hit *Strangers In the Night* appear in ?

  a. *The Oscar*

  b. *A Man Could Get Killed*

  c. *Run For Your Wife*

****

12. What '60s British group included members Roger Greenaway and Roger Cook ?

  a. the Searchers

  b. the Mindbenders

  c. David & Jonathan

Questions 13-16: **SONG HITS**

****

13. What was Jay & the Americans' first U.S. Billboard Top 40 hit ?

   a. *Come A Little Bit Closer*

   b. *She Cried*

   c. *Only In America*

****

14. What was the Rascals' last U.S. Top 20 hit ?

   a. *A Beautiful Morning*

   b. *People Got to Be Free*

   c. *How Can I Be Sure*

****

15. What was the Mamas & the Papas' first single to reach the U.S. Billboard Top 20 record charts ?

   a. *California Dreamin'*

   b. *Monday Monday*

   c. *Creeque Alley*

****

16. What was the Cowsills' last U.S. Top 40 hit ?

   a. *Hair*

   b. *Indian Lake*

   c. *In Need of a Friend*

17. What obscure 1964 group featured future Buffalo Springfield members Richie Furay and Stephen Stills ?

> a. the Au Go–Go Singers
> b. the Richie Furay Four
> c. Stop & Go

****

18. On which nationally televised show did Ssgt. Barry Sadler NOT perform his hit *The Ballad of the Green Berets* ?

> a. *The Glen Campbell Goodtime Hour*
> b. *The Jimmy Dean Show*
> c. *The Ed Sullivan Show*

****

19. Which group sang the title track, *Easy Rider (Let the Wind Pay the Way),* from the 1970 movie *Easy Rider* ?

> a. Tommy James & the Shondells
> b. Iron Butterfly
> c. the Byrds

****

20. What was the last album the Beatles recorded together ?

> a. *Yesterday and Today*
> b. *Abbey Road*
> c. *Let It Be*

Quiz 17

1. b. **Johnny Cowsill** . . . Mousketeer Cubby became drummer for the Carpenters, Mousketeer Dickie Dodd for the Standells . . . Johnny Cowsill, young drummer for the Cowsills, was never a Mousketeer, though he did have the longest tenure as drummer, extending his career with Mike Love's Beach Boys for many years into the 21st century

2. c. *Reach Out of the Darkness* (Friend & Lover) . . . the song's refrain is "Reach out in the darkness" — apparently, the line didn't look good on the record, so the title was changed

3. a. he set his guitar on fire in a bizarre ritual

4. c. Donovan

5. c. *Good Golly Miss Molly,* Little Richard's 1958 hit

6. c. *Come Together* . . . neither the use of the Beatles song nor his bid for governor ever materialized

7. c. *While My Guitar Gently Weeps,* contained on the *White Album*

8. a. 1956

9. b. Jean Terrell

10. a. William Levise, Jr.

11. b. *A Man Could Get Killed*

12. c. **David & Jonathan,** whose version of the Beatles' *Michelle* reached #18 in the U.S. Billboard singles chart in 1966

****

Questions 13-16: SONG HITS

13. b. *She Cried*

14. b. *People Got to Be Free*

15. a. *California Dreamin',* in February, 1966

16. a. *Hair*

****

Questions 17-20: HARDER QUESTIONS

17. a. the Au Go-Go Singers

18. a. *The Glen Campbell Goodtime Hour*

19. b. Iron Butterfly . . . the Byrds performed *The Ballad of Easy Rider*

20. b. *Abbey Road* . . . Though *Let It Be* was released after *Abbey Road,* it was recorded earlier by the group, then totally remixed at a later date by Phil Spector, who had Ringo come in one last time to provide additional drums to three of the tracks

Quiz 18

1. For whom did Paul McCartney write *Hey Jude* ?

    a. a loyal fan

    b. his nephew

    c. John Lennon's son

****

2. Where did the first two members of Procol Harum locate the remaining members for the band ?

    a. at a bar

    b. at a soccer game

    c. through a newspaper ad

****

3. The Band was the backup for which famous rocker in the '60s ?

    a. Bob Dylan

    b. Neil Diamond

    c. Janis Joplin

****

4. Why did Mick Jagger not release his 1968 rock-concert film *Rock 'n' Roll Circus* ?

    a. the film became mired in a legal dispute

    b. he felt it painted too dark an image of the circus

    c. Jagger didn't like the way he looked

5. Tim Hardin reached the Billboard Hot 100 singles chart in 1969 with *Simple Song of Freedom,* a song Bobby Darin wrote for him after he had earlier written a song for Darin. What was the song Tim Hardin wrote for Bobby Darin ?

> a. *Things*
> b. *18 Yellow Roses*
> c. *If I Were a Carpenter*

****

6. What inspired the 5ᵗʰ Dimension to record *Aquarius/Let the Sunshine In* ?

> a. seeing a musical
> b. an earlier version released by another band
> c. a recommendation by their fan club

****

7. Which group leader found success after misunderstanding the Beatles' *Lucy In the Sky With Diamonds* ?

> a. Reg Presley
> b. John Fred
> c. Gary Lewis

****

8. Which of the following groups was NOT an offshoot of the Buffalo Springfield ?

> a. the Flying Burrito Brothers
> b. Crosby, Stills, Nash and Young
> c. Poco

9. Which is the only group whose first album reached #1 on the record charts but who never had another album reach the charts at all ?

    a. the Box Tops

    b. Blind Faith

    c. the Yellow Balloon

****

10. On which label did Bob Dylan record his hits, including *Like A Rolling Stone* ?

    a. Columbia

    b. Capitol

    c. Verve

****

11. Which group featured members including Paul and Art ?

    a. the Righteous Brothers

    b. Simon & Garfunkel

    c. the Walker Brothers

****

12. Which famous singer was born Noah Kaminsky ?

    a. Neil Diamond

    b. Neil Sedaka

    c. Norman Greenbaum

Questions 13-16: SONG HITS

****

13. What was the Raiders' last U.S. Top 40 hit ?

      a. *Birds of a Feather*

      b. *Indian Reservation*

      c. *Let Me*

****

14. What was Peter & Gordon's only U.S. #1 hit ?

      a. *Woman*

      b. *I Go To Pieces*

      c. *A World Without Love*

****

15. What was Donovan's last U.S. Top 40 hit ?

      a. *Goo Goo Barabajagal (Love Is Hot)*

      b. *Atlantis*

      c. *Lalena*

****

16. Which of the following #1 hits charted the longest
for the (Young) Rascals on the U.S. Billboard
singles chart ?

      a. *Groovin'*

      b. *People Got to Be Free*

      c. *Good Lovin'*

HARDER QUESTIONS (17-20): 2 points each
(4 points if you can answer the question without the three choices !)

17. On what melody is Procol Harum's *A Whiter Shade of Pale* based ?

     a. *Bolero*

     b. *Francesca da Rimini*

     c. *Sleepers Awake*

****

18. What song is being referred to in the following by a '60s musicologist: "There has been no song remotely like this one in the . . . history of rock music — strident and bitter, its references blatantly topical."

     a. *Sympathy for the Devil* / Rolling Stones

     b. *My Generation* / Who

     c. *Eve of Destruction* / Barry McGuire

****

19. Donovan often referred to Gypsy Dave in his songs. Who was Gypsy Dave ?

     a. a wandering minstrel who cared for him in his youth

     b. a fellow musician

     c. a fictional character

****

20. What is so special about the leader of the British group Scaffold, who scored with their 1968 British hit *Thank U Very Much* ?

     a. he was an original member of Monty Python's Flying Circus

     b. he was Paul McCartney's brother

     c. he won a multi-million dollar lottery in the same year

Quiz 18

1. c. John Lennon's son . . . the song, originally titled *Hey Jules,* was written to ease son Julian Lennon's pain following the divorce of his famous Beatle-dad from Cynthia Lennon

2. c. through a 1967 ad in the British *Melody Maker* music magazine

3. a. Bob Dylan

4. c. Jagger didn't like the way he looked

5. c. *If I Were a Carpenter,* Darin's last Top 20 hit, in 1966

6. a. seeing *Hair* and being thrilled by the version of *Aquarius,* performed by Ronnie Dyson

7. b. John Fred . . . Thinking the title was *Lucy In Disguise With Diamonds,* his Playboy Band used the faux pas to shortly thereafter produce and record their #1 hit, *Judy In Disguise (With Glasses)*

8. a. the Flying Burrito Brothers

9. b. Blind Faith . . . the group, which included Eric Clapton, Steve Winwood & Ginger Baker, never released another album . . . Yellow Balloon's only LP never reached #1

10. a. Columbia

11. b. Simon & Garfunkel

12. a. Neil Diamond

****

Questions 13-16: SONG HITS

13. a. *Birds of a Feather*

14. c. *A World Without Love,* in 1964

15. a. *Goo Goo Barabajagal (Love Is Hot),* in 1969

16. b. *People Got to Be Free,* #1 for 5 weeks in 1968 (billed as the Rascals); *Groovin'* topped the charts for 4 weeks (billed as the Young Rascals)

****

Questions 17-20: HARDER QUESTIONS

17. c. *Sleepers Awake,* a cantata by Bach

18. c. *Eve of Destruction* / Barry McGuire . . . P.F. Sloan's composition is perhaps even more relevant today!

19. b. a fellow musician who played the kazoo with Donovan in U.K. folk clubs in the mid-'60s

20. b. leader Mike McGear was Paul McCartney's younger brother

Quiz 19

1. In what film was footage from the infamous 1969 Altamont concert shown ?

        a. *Woodstock*

        b. *Performance*

        c. *Gimme Shelter*

****

2. What was the first Billboard Top 40 hit to be listed as by Kenny Rogers & the First Edition ?

a. *Just Dropped In (To See What Condition My Condition Was In)*

b. *But You Know I Love You*

c. *Ruby, Don't Take Your Love to Town*

****

3. What did Jim Morrison die from ?

        a. a heart attack

        b. a heroin overdose

        c. a self-inflicted gunshot

****

4. Which musician was originally sought to sing *Raindrops Keep Fallin' On My Head* for the movie *Butch Cassidy & the Sundance Kid* ?

        a. Gene Pitney

        b. Bob Dylan

        c. Tom Jones

5. What were the missing words in the line "'cause I'm the * * * that named you Sue" that were bleeped out of Johnny Cash's 1969 hit *A Boy Named Sue* ?

    a. son–of–a–b – – – ch

    b. motherf – – – er

    c. a – – hole

****

6. Who joined as lead singer when the Small Faces reformed as the Faces in 1969 ?

    a. Rod Stewart

    b. Jimmy Page

    c. Jeff Beck

****

7. In which hotel did John Lennon & Yoko Ono stay during their famous 1969 protest for world peace called the "Bed–In" ?

    a. Amsterdam Hilton

    b. Waldorf–Astoria

    c. Beverly Wilshire

****

8. What experience affected the Grateful Dead's early music and won the group a different following ?

    a. an encounter with Jimi Hendrix

    b. experimentation with LSD

    c. a religious conversion

9. Who called his band the "first fusion of psychedelia and rhythm & Blues" ?

        a. Eric Clapton

        b. James Brown

        c. Sly Stone

****

10. On which label did Jefferson Airplane record their hits, including *White Rabbit* ?

        a. Columbia

        b. RCA

        c. Uni

****

11. What group consisted of James and Cathy Post ?

        a. Friend & Lover

        b. Peaches & Herb

        c. Gene & Debbe

****

12. Mary O'Brien was the real (birth) name for which of the following British stars ?

        a. Dusty Springfield

        b. Mary Hopkin

        c. Petula Clark

Questions 13-16: SONG HITS

****

13. What was Johnny Rivers' only U.S. #1 hit ?

        a. *Baby I Need Your Lovin'*

        b. *Poor Side of Town*

        c. *Secret Agent Man*

****

14. What was the Vogues' last U.S. Top 20 hit ?

        a. *Magic Town*

        b. *My Special Angel*

        c. *Turn Around, Look At Me*

****

15. What was Tommy James & the Shondells' first U.S. #1 hit ?

        a. *Hanky Panky*

        b. *Crimson & Clover*

        c. *Mony Mony*

****

16. What was the Ohio Express's last U.S. Top 40 hit ?

        a. *Down at Lulu's*

        b. *Chewy Chewy*

        c. *Mercy*

HARDER QUESTIONS (17-20): 2 points each
(4 points if you can answer the question without the three choices !)

17. What did Gary Puckett & the Union Gap first call themselves when they formed in 1967 ?
    a. the Bayonettes
    b. the Outcasts
    c. Gary & the Rebels

****

18. What provoked the writing of the Rascals 1968 hit *People Got to Be Free,* according to the book *Dick Clark's The First 25 Years of Rock & Roll* ?
    a. the Viet Nam war
    b. a run-in with a redneck group
    c. the assassination of Robert Kennedy

****

19. On what variety show did Iron Butterfly make their debut network performance ?
    a. *The Smothers Brothers Comedy Hour*
    b. *The Ed Sullivan Show*
    c. *The Red Skelton Show*

****

20. What was the reason Stephen Stills was turned down when he auditioned for a part in the new television series, *The Monkees* ?
    a. he was a real musician
    b. his accent was too thick
    c. his teeth and hair weren't perfect

Quiz 19

1. c. *Gimme Shelter*
2. c. *Ruby, Don't Take Your Love to Town*
3. a. a heart attack, in Paris, 1971
4. b. Bob Dylan . . . Dylan declined the offer, and B. J. Thomas was asked next
5. a. "son-of-a-bitch," a surprisingly tepid phrase, reflective of the double-standard morality of the time
6. a. Rod Stewart
7. a. Amsterdam Hilton, Room 702
8. b. experimentation with LSD
9. c. Sly Stone, describing his band: Sly & the Family Stone
10. b. RCA
11. a. Friend & Lover
12. a. Dusty Springfield

****

Questions 13-16: SONG HITS

13. b. *Poor Side of Town*, #1 in 1966
14. b. *My Special Angel*
15. a. *Hanky Panky*
16. c. *Mercy*

****

Questions 17-20: HARDER QUESTIONS

17. b. the Outcasts
18. b. According to the book, a run-in with a redneck group in Florida who forced them to leave Fort Pierce because of their long hair precipitated the anthem . . . In addition, as a result of the incident, the Rascals announced that they would not appear on any show that didn't include at least one black act, even turning down an appearance on *The Ed Sullivan Show* as a result . . . Many other sources, however, support the RFK theory . . .
19. c. *The Red Skelton Show,* in 1968, during which time they played the *Iron Butterfly Theme* song
20. c. his teeth and hair weren't perfect . . . but all worked out well when he told a "more suitable" friend about the open audition: Peter Tork

Quiz 20

1. What song was described as singing about "suspicious parents, racing heartbeats, and aching teenage lust" which "captured the sweaty side of teenage romances in parked cars and drive-ins all over America"?

   a. *I Think We're Alone Now* / Tommy James & the Shondells

   b. *Time of the Season* / Zombies

   c. *Let's Live For Today* / Grass Roots

****

2. How did singer Otis Redding die?

   a. in a plane crash

   b. he was shot by a crazed fan

   c. in a house fire

****

3. Whose 4ᵗʰ-of-July White House performance was cancelled because they supposedly appealed to an undesirable segment of America?

   a. the Electric Prunes

   b. the Standells

   c. the Beach Boys

****

4. What was Jimi Hendrix's first released single on Reprise Records?

   a. *Foxy Lady*

   b. *All Along the Watchtower*

   c. *Hey Joe*

5. What 1969 song was later used in a television ad for Maxell tapes, with mis-read lyrics flashed from hand-held poster boards ?

    a. *Wear Your Love Like Heaven*

    b. *Subterranean Homesick Blues*

    c. *The Israelites*

****

6. The Guess Who's first hit, *Shakin' All Over,* was actually released under a former name for the group. What was the group then called ?

    a. G.Q. & the Silvertones

    b. Chad Allen & the Expressions

    c. Randy & the Reflections

****

7. Why did the Cowsills turn down the invitation to star in the new television series *The Partridge Family*?

    a. they felt it would adversely affect their musical career

    b. the producers didn't want the entire family

    c. the family wasn't offered enough money

****

8. What song did Jimmy Page NOT play lead guitar on ?

    a. *Hang on Sloopy* / McCoys

    b. *Gloria* / Them

    c. *It's Not Unusual* / Tom Jones

9. In which city did the Monkees perform their first live concert ?

> a. San Francisco
>
> b. Honolulu
>
> c. Anaheim

****

10. Mark Stein was the lead singer for which group ?

> a. Max Frost & the Troopers
>
> b. Vanilla Fudge
>
> c. Deep Purple

****

11. On which label did Steppenwolf record their hits, including *Magic Carpet Ride* ?

> a. Dunhill
>
> b. Fantasy
>
> c. Reprise

****

12. Which group consisted of members named Denny and Rick ?

> a. the Walker Brothers
>
> b. the Righteous Brothers
>
> c. Zager & Evans

Questions 13-16: **SONG HITS**

****

13. What was Nilsson's first U.S. Billboard Top 40 hit ?

      a. *Without You*

      b. *Everybody's Talkin'*

      c. *Coconut*

****

14. What was Lou Christie's last U.S. Top 40 hit ?

      a. *I'm Gonna Make You Mine*

      b. *Rhapsody In the Rain*

      c. *Lightnin' Strikes*

****

15. *Happy Together* was the Turtles' only #1 hit. What was their 2nd-highest-charting single?

      a. *She'd Rather Be With Me*

      b. *It Ain't Me Babe*

      c. *Elenore*

****

16. What was Glen Campbell's first U.S. Billboard Top 40 hit ?

      a. *Wichita Lineman*

      b. *Galveston*

      c. *By the Time I Get to Phoenix*

HARDER QUESTIONS (17-20): 2 points each
(4 points if you can answer the question without the three choices !)

17. What was the original name of the group whose members were Felix, Eddie, Gene and Dino ?
   - a. the Young Rascals
   - b. the Rascals
   - c. the Little Rascals

****

18. Which of the following groups did NOT have a song featured in the 1967 movie *The Savage Seven* ?
   - a. Steppenwolf
   - b. Iron Butterfly
   - c. Cream

****

19. What was the Creedence Clearwater Revival's hit *Who'll Stop the Rain* an allegory about ?
   - a. the band's internal conflicts
   - b. the Viet Nam war
   - c. the destruction of the Earth's atmosphere

****

20. What flavor of ice cream did Baskin-Robbins create to commemorate the Beatles' 1964 American tour ?
   - a. Yeah Yeah Peppermint
   - b. She Loves Spumone
   - c. Beatle Nut

Quiz 20

1. a. *I Think We're Alone Now* / Tommy James & the Shondells
2. a. in a plane crash, in 1967
3. c. the Beach Boys, in 1983 . . . Secretary of the Interior, James Watt, preferred having Wayne Newton perform
4. c. *Hey Joe*
5. c. *The Israelites,* with humorous lyrics, such as for the title: "My ears are alight"
6. b. Chad Allen & the Expressions . . . Chad Allen sang lead vocals on the track
7. b. the producers didn't want the entire family . . . they wanted Shirley Jones to play the mother's role
8. a. *Hang on Sloopy* / McCoys
9. b. Honolulu, on December 3, 1966
10. b. Vanilla Fudge
11. a. Dunhill
12. c. Zager & Evans (Denny Zager & Rick Evans)

****

Questions 13-16: SONG HITS

13. b. *Everybody's Talkin'*
14. a. *I'm Gonna Make You Mine,* in 1969
15. a. *She'd Rather Be With Me*
16. c. *By the Time I Get to Phoenix*

****

Questions 17-20: HARDER QUESTIONS

17. b. the Rascals . . . their original 1964 nightclub name was Rascals, then changed to Young Rascals when signed to Atlantic Records, then changed back to Rascals in 1968 . . . The group wearing the knickerbockers was the Rascals . . . they no longer wore the knickerbocker outfits after they signed with Atlantic as the Young Rascals, but nonetheless, the first album on Atlantic Records shows them wearing knickerbockers !
18. a. Steppenwolf
19. b. the Viet Nam war
20. c. Beatle Nut

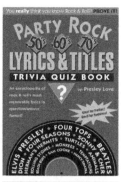

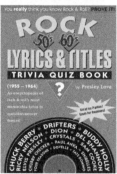
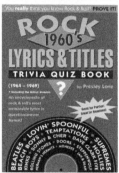
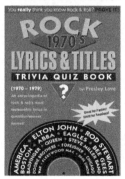
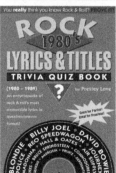

Available on Amazon.com